Tiger Oak Publications
Editor: Susan Bonne
Editorial Assistant: Beth Dooley
Book Design: Alicia Nammacher
Layout and Design: Courtney Colwell
Publisher: R. Craig Bednar

Land O'Lakes, Inc.
Publisher: Peter Theisen
Publications Manager: Mary Sue Peterson
Food Editor: Cindy Manwarren

Published by Tiger Oak Publications
251 1st Avenue North, Suite 401
Minneapolis, Minnesota 55401

First printing: September 1999
Printed in U.S.A.

ISBN 0-9663558-2-2

TIGER OAK
PUBLICATIONS

Cookies

Favorite recipes from the Land O'Lakes Test Kitchens

Land O'Lakes

A History of Fresh Ideas

A History of Fresh Ideas Over seventy-five years ago, on the rolling grassland dairy farms of Minnesota and Wisconsin, farmers united to form the cooperative creamery that became Land O'Lakes. Driven by a desire to provide consumers with the very best butter possible, they created many innovations in the industry, including making their butter from sweet cream only—an idea that assured butter quality and literally changed America's eating habits.

Home and professional cooks alike responded with enthusiasm, turning to Land O'Lakes for more ideas in using its pure, sweet cream butter. Since 1949, the Land O'Lakes Test Kitchens has been developing recipes used and loved by generations. As we celebrate the Test Kitchens' 50th anniversary, we're proud to bring you this all-new chapter in home cooking with Land O'Lakes.

Fine quality ingredients are key to any efforts in the kitchen. After all, if you are taking the time to cook from scratch, you want delicious results. With fresh-tasting additions like butter, cheese and sour cream, time-tested recipes and your own creativity and skill, cooking and baking become the ultimate simple pleasure. Enjoy!

Questions About Baking?

Since 1990, Land O'Lakes Bakeline operators have been helping home cooks turn out the best baked goods possible. If you have a question about baking or cooking, call

1-800-782-9606

from November 1 through December 24, 8 a.m. to 6 p.m. (CST).

ABOVE: LAND O'LAKES TRUCKS OUTSIDE THE ORGANIZATION'S CHICAGO OFFICES CIRCA 1946 AWAIT THEIR CARGO OF DAIRY PRODUCTS. BELOW: THE BUTTER BOX AT RIGHT WAS THE FIRST TO BEAR THE LAND O'LAKES NAME IN THE MID-1920s; WITHIN A FEW YEARS, IT WAS REDESIGNED TO SHOW MORE OF THE INDIAN MAIDEN.

Chocolate Chip Thumbprints, page 52
(On the cover: Buttery Jam Tarts, page 94)

Contents

Cookies

Cookies call us to the kitchen with comforting aromas and the promise of something sweet. Easily made, quickly baked, cookies, for many of us, were our first taste of real baking. Guided by mothers, grandmothers, sisters and aunts, we cut stars, painted gingerbread shapes, and bit into warm chocolate chip cookies fresh off the sheet. Today, although our schedules are hectic and our days fast-paced, cookie-baking retains its simple appeal. It connects us to our past, yet tempts us to try new flavors and techniques.

At Land O'Lakes, we've been baking for generations, and have more than 700 cookie recipes in our collection. In this volume, we feature our best classic, elaborate and easy recipes; cookies for morning coffee, afternoon tea, bake sales and holiday boxes. Whatever recipes you choose to create, cookies are always in season and right in style.

Chocolate Almond Wafers, page 34

With years of test kitchen know-how and the wisdom gleaned from working with home cooks, Land O'Lakes is a great baker's resource. Whether you're a seasoned pro or an eager beginner, this book allows you to indulge your imagination and enjoy the sweet rewards.

Ingredients

DAIRY AND EGGS

Be sure eggs and dairy products (sour cream, butter, cream and milk) are fresh by checking the sell-by dates on the containers. A note of caution: Don't nibble on dough that contains uncooked eggs. Salmonella, a serious, potentially fatal food poisoning, can be contracted by eating raw whole eggs. Pasteurized raw whole eggs or egg product substitutes are safe to eat in unbaked cookies.

notes on nuts

Toast shelled nuts by spreading them evenly on a shallow baking pan and placing in a 325° oven for 5 to 10 minutes, stirring occasionally until lightly browned.

CHOCOLATE

Taste the chocolate used in baking — it should not taste stale or "off." Sometimes chocolate stored at uneven temperatures develops a "bloom" (gray-white film) caused by cocoa butter rising to the surface. Bloom does not affect the flavor or quality of the chocolate.

To Melt Chocolate:

On the stove Break the chocolate into pieces or small chunks, then place in the top pan of a double boiler or small saucepan. If using a double boiler, do not allow the water in the lower pan to touch the top pan. Whichever method you use, keep the heat very low to prevent burning and stir the chocolate constantly. Once the chocolate is melted, immediately remove from the heat and stir again until it is smooth.

In the microwave Put chunks of chocolate in a microwave-safe dish, cover, then microwave on High for one minute. Stir, return to microwave for 30 seconds, then remove and stir again. Repeat this step just until the chocolate is melted.

FLOUR

These recipes call for all-purpose flour—a blend of select hard and soft wheat flours that gives the proper structure to cookies. Today's flours are pre-sifted, so you won't need to sift again. You can use either bleached or unbleached all-purpose flours; bleaching simply means the flour has been whitened, either by natural aging or a chemical process.

To Measure Flour:

Gently spoon the flour into a dry-measuring cup and level the top with the straight edge of a metal spatula or knife. Don't pack the flour into the cup or tap it with the spatula or on the counter to level; you'll end up with too much.

LEAVENING

Baking powder or baking soda, the agents that make cookies rise, are not interchangeable. Check the containers' expiration dates to be sure you're using fresh leaveners or your cookies and bars will literally fall flat.

To test baking powder, add 1 teaspoon to $1/3$ cup hot water. If it bubbles vigorously, the baking powder is still good.

NUTS

Taste nuts before adding them to a recipe. Nuts can turn rancid and taste horrible if old or poorly stored. You may substitute any nut for those called for in most of these recipes.

SWEETENERS

Brown sugar is a mix of granulated white sugar and molasses. In our recipes, the "light" variety may be used interchangeably with the "dark," which has a deeper, richer flavor. To measure, spoon into a dry-measuring cup, packing down firmly until level with the top of the cup.

White sugar The most common sweetener, it should be measured by dipping out of the container with a dry-measuring cup. The amount should then be leveled with a metal spatula or straight-edged knife.

Powdered sugar is finely ground granulated white sugar with a little cornstarch. It cannot be used interchangeably with granulated sugar. To measure, lightly spoon into a dry-measuring cup and level the top with a spatula or knife.

Liquid sweeteners—corn syrup, honey and molasses—all give different, distinctive flavors and textures to cookies. Measure using the following method: Lightly butter or spray the inside of a glass measuring cup with cooking spray (this helps keep the sticky liquids from clinging to the cup). Pour the syrup into the cup on a flat surface and read the measurement at eye level.

sweet sense

To keep brown sugar soft and moist, store it in an airtight container. If it becomes hard or lumpy, its texture can be restored by placing a slice of bread in the container. Replace the bread in one or two days.

BUTTER

There is no substitute for real butter. It creates cookies with a tender texture and rich flavor. Salted and unsalted butter can be used interchangeably in recipes. Do not use lowfat or reduced-fat spreads for baking. They contain more moisture than butter and can result in cookies that are tough and less tasty. Cookies made with lower-fat substitutes also tend to stick to the cookie sheet and stale quickly.

Extracts Vanilla extract is the most common; be sure to use real vanilla rather than an imitation flavoring. Try other extracts such as almond, maple, lemon or orange in butter or sugar cookies.

best butter

1. Always refrigerate butter in its original wrapping, in its original package. 2. Store in the coldest part of the refrigerator, not in the "butter keeper" in the door. Butter will retain its freshness for four months; for longer storage, freeze in the carton.

Softened butter
Most recipes call for softened butter, which will blend smoothly with sugar and other ingredients. Remove the butter from the refrigerator and let stand at room temperature for 30 to 40 minutes. Do not let butter become too soft, or the dough will be overly soft, causing the cookies to spread too much while baking.

Softened butter should give gently when pressed with your finger, but not appear to be melting on the plate. To soften butter quickly, try this tip from Julia Child: Strike a stick of cold butter several times with a rolling pin.

Butter Measurements			
2 cups	= 4 sticks	= 1 pound	
1 cup	= 2 sticks	= ½ pound	
½ cup	= 1 stick	= ¼ pound	
¼ cup	= ½ stick	= 4 tablespoons	

Cookie Sheet Secrets

Use heavy-gauge, shiny aluminum cookie sheets with very low sides or no sides at all. Dark baking sheets absorb heat and may cause cookie bottoms to over-brown.

Jelly-roll pans (15 x 10 x 1-inch baking pans) will work for bar cookies but not for drop, rolled or sliced cookies, because these won't bake evenly in a pan with an edge. If you must use a jelly-roll pan for a cookie sheet, turn it over and bake your cookies on the bottom.

Insulated baking sheets tend to heat up too slowly and cookies may become coarse-textured and dry. Bar cookies may not be done in the center.

Cookie sheets must be at least two inches narrower and shorter than the oven.

Always let cookie sheets cool before placing dough on them. Drop, slice or cut-out cookies will spread excessively and brown too much around the edges if put on a hot cookie sheet. Just add an extra sheet to the rotation to give hot cookie sheets a chance to cool off.

For cookies that are delicately browned, bake one sheet of cookies at a time on the center oven rack.

MAKE-AHEAD DOUGH

Many cookie doughs can be refrigerated, and most freeze well. Package the dough in airtight containers. Store it in the refrigerator up to two days or freeze it up to three months. Thaw the dough in the refrigerator until it is just soft enough to use.

COOLING OFF

Cookies should be removed from the sheet immediately after baking (unless the recipe specifies otherwise) and set on a rack, about 1 to 2 inches high. This allows air to circulate and cool the cookie bottoms—otherwise, they'll become soggy instead of crisp.

STORING COOKIES

Always allow cookies and bars to cool completely before you store them.

To Store:

Soft Cookies Placing a piece of waxed paper between each layer, stack cookies in an airtight container. If the cookies begin to dry out, put a slice of bread on a piece of waxed paper, then place inside the storage container. Replace the bread every day or two.

Crisp Cookies Store in a container with a loose lid, unless you live in a humid climate. If humidity is high, keep the cookies in a container with a tight-fitting lid.

Frosted Cookies Stack frosted cookies in layers with waxed paper separating each layer. To avoid smudging the frosting, don't stack more than three layers of cookies per container.

FREEZING COOKIES

To freeze unfrosted cookies, layer them in a freezer-safe container or resealable plastic food bag, placing waxed paper or aluminum foil between each layer. Do not freeze frosted cookies: instead, freeze unfrosted and frost when thawed and ready to serve.

When freezing any cookies, remember to label the bags with the date and contents. Most cookies will freeze well for up to six months.

To thaw, remove cookies from freezer, loosely cover and allow them to stand at room temperature for 15 to 20 minutes.

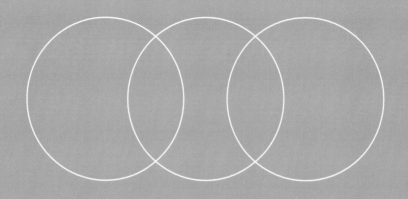

Spoon Drop

Freshly baked cookies and a glass of cold milk.
Imagine this pairing and it's often a tasty drop
cookie that comes to mind. This chapter's
selection of favorites features hearty classics and
delicate confections—all made using the most
basic of tools: two spoons and a cookie sheet.

Maple Walnut Creams

Technique

Use two regular tableware spoons to drop the dough. Scoop the dough with one spoon and then push it onto the cookie sheet with the other.

To get the same size drop cookie every time, try using a small ice cream scoop. Try to make rounded shapes about an inch in diameter.

If the cookies spread too much while baking, cover the bowl of dough with plastic food wrap and refrigerate for about 30 minutes before baking.

Maple Walnut Creams

A wonderful complement to coffee or tea, these frosted cookies will keep up to a week if properly stored.

Preparation time: 1 hour
Baking time: 10 minutes
Cooling time: 15 minutes

[3 dozen cookies]

COOKIE
1   cup firmly packed brown sugar
½   cup LAND O LAKES®
     Butter, softened
½   cup LAND O LAKES®
     Sour Cream
1   egg
1   teaspoon maple flavoring
2   cups all-purpose flour
½   teaspoon baking powder
½   teaspoon baking soda
½   teaspoon salt
1   cup chopped walnuts

FROSTING
2   cups powdered sugar
2   tablespoons LAND O LAKES®
     Sour Cream
1   tablespoon maple flavoring
1-2 tablespoons milk

1. Heat oven to 375°. Combine brown sugar, butter, sour cream, egg and maple flavoring in large mixer bowl. Beat at medium speed, scraping bowl often, until creamy (1 to 2 minutes).

2. Reduce speed to low; add all remaining cookie ingredients *except* walnuts. Beat until well mixed (1 to 2 minutes). Stir in walnuts by hand.

3. Drop dough by rounded teaspoonfuls 2 inches apart onto ungreased cookie sheets. Bake for 10 to 13 minutes or until golden brown. Cool completely.

4. Combine all frosting ingredients *except* milk in small mixer bowl. Beat at low speed, scraping bowl often and gradually adding enough milk for desired spreading consistency. Frost cooled cookies.

Nutrition Facts (1 cookie): Calories 130; Protein 2 g; Carbohydrate 19 g; Dietary Fiber 0 g; Fat 6 g; Cholesterol 15 mg; Sodium 85 mg

TIP To store these or other frosted cookies, allow the frosting to set. Stack the cookies in an airtight container, layering with waxed paper to separate each layer. Don't stack more than three layers of cookies per container. If the cookies begin to dry out, place a slice of bread on a piece of waxed paper and set this in the container. Replace the bread every day or two as needed.

Black Walnut Macaroons

Black walnuts give this coconut confection its distinctive flavor.

Preparation time: 35 minutes
Baking time: 18 minutes

[3 dozen cookies]

2	egg whites
1	teaspoon vanilla
½	cup sugar
2½	cups flaked coconut
1	(2-ounce) package (½ cup) chopped black walnuts
2	tablespoons all-purpose flour

1. Heat oven to 300°. Combine egg whites and vanilla in small mixer bowl. Beat at high speed until foamy. Continue beating, gradually adding sugar, until soft peaks form (3 to 5 minutes). Gently stir in coconut, walnuts and flour by hand.

2. Drop dough by rounded teaspoonfuls 2 inches apart onto parchment-lined cookie sheets. Bake for 18 to 22 minutes or until lightly browned and tops are no longer moist. Let stand 2 minutes; remove from cookie sheets. Cool completely.

Nutrition Facts (1 cookie): Calories 60; Protein 1 g; Carbohydrate 6 g; Dietary Fiber 0 g; Fat 3 g Cholesterol 0 mg; Sodium 20 mg

TIP If you cannot find black walnuts, substitute regular walnuts. Lightly toast the walnuts in the oven at 350° for 7 to 10 minutes.

TIP Most nuts can be purchased shelled or unshelled. When buying unshelled nuts, choose nuts that are heavy for their size, and look for shells that have no cracks, holes or visible decay. The nut should not "rattle" inside the shell when shaken. When time is at a premium, ready-to-use shelled nuts are more convenient. These should be uniform in both size and color, with a fresh, firm appearance. Because all nuts are high in fat and therefore prone to rancidity, store them in an airtight container in a cool, dry place for no more than 3 to 4 months. Nuts can be frozen for up to 6 months in a resealable plastic freezer bag.

[kitchen notes]

Keep a batch or two of your favorite cookie dough in the freezer. It will be ready to bake on a moment's notice. Simply prepare the cookie dough as directed.

Drop dough onto a cookie sheet by spoonfuls and freeze until firm. Remove the mounds of dough from the cookie sheet and place in a resealable plastic freezer bag.

Store in the freezer. When ready to bake, remove the frozen mounds of dough from bag, place on a cookie sheet and pop in the oven (you may need to adjust the baking time slightly).

Apricot Butter Cookies

Light and tender, these cookies boast chopped apricots and pecans.

Preparation time: 1 hour 20 minutes
Baking time: 11 minutes
Cooling time: 15 minutes

[6 dozen cookies]

COOKIE

1½ cups powdered sugar
1   cup LAND O LAKES®
     Butter, softened
1   egg
½   teaspoon vanilla
2   cups all-purpose flour
1   teaspoon baking soda
1   teaspoon cream of tartar
1   cup coarsely chopped
     pecans, toasted
1   (6-ounce) package chopped
     dried apricots, *reserve* ⅓ *cup*

     Powdered sugar

1. Heat oven to 350°. Combine 1½ cups powdered sugar and 1 cup butter in large mixer bowl. Beat at medium speed, scraping bowl often, until well mixed (1 to 2 minutes). Add egg and ½ teaspoon vanilla; continue beating until well mixed (1 minute). Reduce speed to low; add flour, baking soda and cream of tartar. Beat until well mixed (1 to 2 minutes). Stir in pecans and apricots by hand.

2. Drop dough by rounded teaspoonfuls 2 inches apart onto ungreased cookie sheets. Bake for 11 to 15 minutes or until light golden brown. Sprinkle with powdered sugar while warm and again when cool.

Nutrition Facts (1 cookie): Calories 60; Protein 1 g; Carbohydrate 7 g; Dietary Fiber 0 g; Fat 4 g; Cholesterol 10 mg; Sodium 45 mg

VARIATION

Frosted Apricot Butter Cookies
Prepare cookies as directed *except* frost cooled cookies with the following recipe:

FROSTING

2¼ cups powdered sugar
¼   cup LAND O LAKES®
     Butter, softened
½   teaspoon vanilla
3-4 tablespoons milk

Combine powdered sugar, butter, vanilla and enough milk for desired spreading consistency in small mixer bowl. Beat at medium speed, scraping bowl often, until well mixed (1 to 2 minutes).

Coconut Oatmeal Crisps

Coconut, oats and rice cereal make these tender cookies crisp. These take well to additions like dried fruit or chocolate baking pieces.

Preparation time: 1 hour
Baking time: 13 minutes

[4 dozen cookies]

3½ cups all-purpose flour
2   cups LAND O LAKES® Butter,
     softened
1   cup sugar
1   cup firmly packed brown sugar
1   egg
1   teaspoon baking soda
½   teaspoon salt
1   cup crisp rice cereal
1   cup flaked coconut
1   cup quick-cooking oats
½   cup chopped walnuts *or*
     pecans

1. Heat oven to 350°. Combine all ingredients *except* rice cereal, coconut, oats and walnuts in large mixer bowl. Beat at low speed, scraping bowl often, until well mixed (2 to 3 minutes). Stir in all remaining ingredients by hand.

2. Drop dough by rounded tablespoonfuls 2 inches apart onto ungreased cookie sheets. Bake for 13 to 16 minutes or until lightly browned.

Nutrition Facts (1 cookie): Calories 160; Protein 2 g; Carbohydrate 18 g; Dietary Fiber 1 g; Fat 9 g; Cholesterol 25 mg; Sodium 135 mg

Apricot Butter Cookies

Homestyle Oatmeal Cookies

These tasty, chewy cookies are a family favorite.

Preparation time: 50 minutes
Baking time: 8 minutes

[4 dozen cookies]

3	cups quick-cooking oats
2	cups firmly packed brown sugar
1	cup LAND O LAKES® Butter, softened
2	eggs
1	teaspoon baking soda
1	teaspoon ground cinnamon
2	teaspoons vanilla
½	teaspoon salt
1¾	cups all-purpose flour
1½	cups raisins

1. Heat oven to 375°. Combine all ingredients *except* flour and raisins in large mixer bowl. Beat at low speed, scraping bowl often, until well mixed (1 to 2 minutes). Add flour; continue beating until well mixed (1 to 2 minutes). Stir in raisins by hand.

2. Drop dough by rounded teaspoonfuls 2 inches apart onto greased cookie sheets. Bake for 8 to 10 minutes or until edges are lightly browned.

Nutrition Facts (1 cookie): Calories 120; Protein 2 g; Carbohydrate 19 g; Dietary Fiber 3 g; Fat 4 g Cholesterol 20 mg; Sodium 90 mg

Caramel-Iced Pumpkin Cookies

Try these spice cookies with a glass of fresh, crisp apple cider.

Preparation time: 1 hour 20 minutes
Baking time: 10 minutes
Cooling time: 15 minutes

[6 dozen cookies]

COOKIE

1	cup LAND O LAKES® Butter, softened
1	cup sugar
1	(15-ounce) can pumpkin
1	egg
1	teaspoon vanilla
2	cups flour
1	teaspoon baking powder
1	teaspoon baking soda
1	teaspoon salt
1	teaspoon ground cinnamon
½	teaspoon ground ginger
1	cup finely chopped pecans, toasted

ICING

½	cup firmly packed brown sugar
¼	cup evaporated milk
3	tablespoons LAND O LAKES® Butter
¾	teaspoon vanilla
1	cup powdered sugar

1. Heat oven to 350°. Combine 1 cup butter and sugar in large mixer bowl. Beat at medium speed, scraping bowl often, until creamy (1 to 2 minutes). Add pumpkin, egg and vanilla; continue beating until well mixed (1 to 2 minutes).

2. Reduce speed to low; add flour, baking powder, baking soda, salt, cinnamon and ginger. Beat until well mixed (1 to 2 minutes). Stir in pecans by hand.

3. Drop dough by rounded teaspoonfuls 1 inch apart onto ungreased cookie sheets. Bake for 10 to 13 minutes or until edges of cookies are lightly browned. Cool 1 minute; remove from cookie sheets. Cool completely.

4. Meanwhile, combine all icing ingredients *except* powdered sugar in medium saucepan. Cook over medium-high heat, stirring constantly, until mixture comes to a full boil (3 to 5 minutes). Remove from heat; cool 10 minutes. Stir in powdered sugar. Frost cooled cookies.

Nutrition Facts (1 cookie): Calories 80; Protein 1 g; Carbohydrate 10 g; Dietary Fiber 0 g; Fat 4.5 g; Cholesterol 10 mg; Sodium 100 mg

Who doesn't love chocolate? Keep semi-sweet baking chips on hand to create simple, irresistible glazes (like the one that adorns these crispy cookies).

Crisp Browned Butter Cookies

Browned butter gives these cookies a wonderful, nutty flavor.

Preparation time: 45 minutes
Cooling time: 15 minutes
Baking time: 6 minutes

[3½ dozen cookies]

⅓	cup LAND O LAKES® Butter
½	cup sugar
1	egg
1	teaspoon vanilla
1	cup all-purpose flour
¼	teaspoon baking powder
⅛	teaspoon salt

1. Heat oven to 400°. Cook butter in 1-quart saucepan over medium heat until very lightly browned (5 to 7 minutes). Pour browned butter in medium mixer bowl; cool 15 minutes.

2. Add sugar, egg and vanilla. Beat at medium speed, scraping bowl often, until mixture thickens and becomes lighter in color (1 to 2 minutes). Reduce speed to low; add all remaining ingredients. Beat until well mixed (1 to 2 minutes). (Dough will be soft.)

3. Drop dough by ½ teaspoonfuls 2 inches apart onto ungreased cookie sheet. Flatten dough to ¼-inch thickness with bottom of buttered glass dipped in sugar. Bake for 6 to 9 minutes or until edges are golden brown.

Nutrition Facts (1 cookie): Calories 35; Protein 0 g; Carbohydrate 5 g; Dietary Fiber 0 g; Fat 2 g; Cholesterol 10 mg; Sodium 25 mg

VARIATION To dress up these cookies, drizzle melted semi-sweet chocolate over them as a final touch.

TIP To brown butter, use very low heat, and watch the butter very, very, closely. Remove pan from heat as soon as butter begins to turn golden—do not allow the butter to actually darken to brown.

Lemon Frosted Ginger Cookies

Simple lemon frosting complements this soft ginger cookie.

Preparation time: 1 hour
Baking time: 8 minutes
Cooling time: 15 minutes

[4 dozen cookies]

COOKIE

½ cup sugar
½ cup LAND O LAKES® Butter, softened
1 egg
½ cup light molasses
½ cup hot water
2⅓ cups all-purpose flour
1 teaspoon baking soda
1 teaspoon ground ginger
½ teaspoon ground cinnamon
¼ teaspoon salt
¼ teaspoon ground cloves

FROSTING

2 cups powdered sugar
¼ cup LAND O LAKES® Butter, softened
2 teaspoons grated lemon zest
2-3 tablespoons milk

Grated lemon zest, if desired

1. Heat oven to 375°. Combine sugar, ½ cup butter and egg in large mixer bowl. Beat at medium speed, scraping bowl often, until well mixed (2 to 3 minutes).

2. Reduce speed to low; add molasses and water. Beat until well mixed (1 to 2 minutes). Add all remaining cookie ingredients; continue beating until well mixed (1 to 2 minutes). (Mixture will resemble heavy cake batter.)

3. Drop dough by rounded teaspoonfuls 2 inches apart onto greased cookie sheets. Bake for 8 to 10 minutes or until set. Cool completely.

4. Combine powdered sugar, ¼ cup butter and 2 teaspoons lemon zest in small mixer bowl. Beat at medium speed, scraping bowl often and gradually adding enough milk for desired spreading consistency. Frost cooled cookies. Sprinkle lemon zest on top, if desired.

Nutrition Facts (1 cookie): Calories 90; Protein 1 g; Carbohydrate 14 g; Dietary Fiber 0 g; Fat 3 g; Cholesterol 10 mg; Sodium 70 mg

Cashew Butter Cookies

Cashews and honey make a delicious pair in this rich cookie.

Preparation time: 1 hour
Baking time: 6 minutes

[4½ dozen cookies]

¾ cup LAND O LAKES® Butter, softened
½ cup firmly packed brown sugar
½ cup honey
1 egg
2 cups all-purpose flour
¾ teaspoon baking soda
½ teaspoon baking powder
1 cup chopped salted cashews

Salted cashew halves

1. Heat oven to 375°. Combine butter, brown sugar, honey and egg in large mixer bowl. Beat at medium speed, scraping bowl often, until creamy (2 to 3 minutes). Reduce speed to low; add all remaining ingredients *except* chopped cashews and cashew halves. Beat until well mixed (1 to 2 minutes). Stir in chopped cashews by hand.

2. Drop dough by rounded teaspoonfuls 2 inches apart onto ungreased cookie sheets. Top each cookie with cashew half. Bake for 6 to 9 minutes or until golden brown.

Nutrition Facts (1 cookie): Calories 80; Protein 1 g; Carbohydrate 9 g; Dietary Fiber 0 g; Fat 4 g; Cholesterol 10 mg; Sodium 70 mg

Lemon Frosted Ginger Cookies

Nutty Chocolate Chunk Cookies

Chock full of big chunks of chocolate, these are a chip off the classic.

Preparation time: 45 minutes
Baking time: 9 minutes

[3 dozen cookies]

1	cup LAND O LAKES® Butter, softened
¾	cup firmly packed brown sugar
½	cup sugar
1	egg
1½	teaspoons vanilla
2¼	cups all-purpose flour
1	teaspoon baking soda
½	teaspoon salt
1	cup coarsely chopped walnuts
1	(8-ounce) bar milk chocolate, cut into ¼-inch pieces

1. Heat oven to 375°. Combine butter, brown sugar, sugar, egg and vanilla in large mixer bowl. Beat at medium speed, scraping bowl often, until creamy (1 to 2 minutes). Reduce speed to low; add flour, baking soda and salt. Beat until well mixed (1 to 2 minutes). Stir in walnuts and chocolate by hand.

2. Drop dough by rounded table-spoonfuls 2 inches apart onto ungreased cookie sheets. Bake for 9 to 11 minutes or until lightly browned. Let stand 1 minute; remove from cookie sheets.

Nutrition Facts (1 cookie): Calories 160; Protein 2 g; Carbohydrate 17 g; Dietary Fiber 1 g; Fat 9 g Cholesterol 20 mg; Sodium 120 mg

TIP Create different cookies by varying the combinations. Try:
- White chocolate chunks and macadamia nuts
- Milk chocolate chunks and peanuts
- Chocolate-coated raisins and dark chocolate chunks

Frosted Mocha Cookies

A rich chocolate cookie with a coffee kick, these make a fine after-dinner nibble.

Preparation time: 1 hour 15 minutes
Baking time: 8 minutes

[5 dozen cookies]

COOKIE

1⅔	cups sugar
⅔	cup LAND O LAKES® Butter, softened
⅓	cup brewed coffee, cooled
¼	cup coffee-flavored liqueur*
2	eggs
2	(1-ounce) squares unsweet-ened baking chocolate, melted
2	teaspoons vanilla
2¾	cups all-purpose flour
2	teaspoons baking powder
¾	teaspoon salt
¼	teaspoon ground cinnamon

FROSTING

3	tablespoons LAND O LAKES® Butter, softened
3	cups powdered sugar
2	tablespoons coffee-flavored liqueur*
3-4	tablespoons brewed coffee

1. Heat oven to 350°. Combine sugar, ⅔ cup butter, coffee, ¼ cup liqueur, eggs, melted chocolate and vanilla in large mixer bowl. Beat at medium speed, scraping bowl often, until creamy (2 to 3 minutes). Reduce speed to low; add all remaining cookie ingredients. Beat until well mixed (1 to 2 minutes).

2. Drop dough by rounded teaspoonfuls 2 inches apart onto ungreased cookie sheets. Bake for 8 to 12 minutes or until set. Cool 1 minute before removing from cookie sheets.

3. Meanwhile, combine all frosting ingredients *except* coffee in medium mixer bowl. Beat at low speed, scraping bowl often and gradually adding enough coffee for desired spreading consistency. Frost cooled cookies. If desired, drizzle with melted chocolate chips.

Nutrition Facts (1 cookie): Calories 100; Protein 1 g; Carbohydrate 16 g; Dietary Fiber 0 g; Fat 3 g; Cholesterol 15 mg; Sodium 70 mg

* Substitute brewed strong coffee

Homestyle Oatmeal Cookies (in jar), page 20
and Nutty Chocolate Chunk Cookies

Honey Gems

The term "gem" is often used for cookies that resemble precious little cakes. These are moist, thanks to the honey, and loaded with good things— oatmeal, wheat germ and sesame seeds.

Preparation time: 45 minutes
Baking time: 8 minutes

[4 dozen cookies]

COOKIE

1½ cups all-purpose flour
⅔   cup LAND O LAKES®
    Butter, softened
½   cup quick-cooking oats
½   cup honey
¼   cup sesame seeds
¼   cup wheat germ
¼   cup orange juice
1   egg
1   tablespoon grated orange zest
1   teaspoon vanilla
½   teaspoon salt
½   teaspoon baking soda

FROSTING

¾   cup powdered sugar
¼   cup LAND O LAKES® Butter,
    softened
1   teaspoon grated orange zest
2   teaspoons orange juice

1. Heat oven to 350°. Combine all cookie ingredients in large mixer bowl. Beat at low speed, scraping bowl often, until well mixed (1 to 2 minutes).

2. Drop dough by rounded teaspoonfuls 2 inches apart onto ungreased cookie sheets. Bake for 8 to 12 minutes or until edges are lightly browned.

3. Combine powdered sugar, ¼ cup butter, 1 teaspoon orange zest and 2 teaspoons orange juice in small mixer bowl. Beat at medium speed, scraping bowl often, until creamy (1 to 2 minutes). Frost warm cookies.

Nutrition Facts (1 cookie): Calories 80; Protein 1 g; Carbohydrate 9 g; Dietary Fiber 0 g; Fat 4 g; Cholesterol 15 mg; Sodium 75 mg

Chocolate-Drizzled Lime Cookies

The tropical tastes of coconut and lime come together in this crisp sugar cookie.

Preparation time: 45 minutes
Baking time: 7 minutes
Cooling time: 15 minutes

[4 dozen cookies]

COOKIE

2¾ cups all-purpose flour
1½ cups sugar
1   cup LAND O LAKES®
    Butter, softened
¾   cup flaked coconut
2   eggs
1   tablespoon grated lime zest
3   tablespoons lime juice
1½ teaspoons cream of tartar
1   teaspoon baking soda
¼   teaspoon salt

DRIZZLE

½   cup semi-sweet real
    chocolate chips
2   tablespoons shortening

1. Heat oven to 400°. Combine all cookie ingredients in large mixer bowl. Beat at low speed, scraping bowl often, until well mixed (1 to 2 minutes).

2. Drop dough by rounded teaspoonfuls 2 inches apart onto ungreased cookie sheets. Bake for 7 to 10 minutes or until edges are lightly browned. Remove from cookie sheets; cool completely.

3. Melt chocolate chips and shortening in 1-quart saucepan over medium heat, stirring constantly, until smooth (2 to 3 minutes). Drizzle chocolate over cooled cookies.

Nutrition Facts (1 cookie): Calories 110; Protein 1 g; Carbohydrate 13 g; Dietary Fiber 0 g; Fat 6 g; Cholesterol 20 mg; Sodium 80 mg

Craving a taste of the past? Cookies sweetened with ingredients like honey, applesauce and raisins have a moist, chewy quality that is both substantial and satisfying, while not overly sweet.

Applesauce Raisin Spice Cookies

In this old-time spice cookie, applesauce lends moistness and taste, while whole wheat flour adds texture and nutrients.

Preparation time: 45 minutes
Baking time: 9 minutes

[6 dozen cookies]

2	cups all-purpose flour
1	cup whole-wheat flour
1	teaspoon baking soda
1½	teaspoons ground cinnamon
½	teaspoon salt
½	teaspoon ground ginger
¼	teaspoon ground allspice
1½	cups firmly packed brown sugar
1	cup LAND O LAKES® Butter, softened
1	cup unsweetened applesauce
2	eggs
1½	cups raisins

Powdered sugar, if desired

1. Heat oven to 375°. Combine flours, baking soda, cinnamon, salt, ginger and allspice in medium bowl; set aside.

2. Combine brown sugar and butter in large mixer bowl. Beat at medium speed, scraping bowl often, until creamy (1 to 2 minutes). Add applesauce and eggs; continue beating until well mixed (1 minute). Reduce speed to low. Beat, gradually adding flour mixture, until well mixed (1 to 2 minutes). Stir in raisins by hand.

3. Drop dough by rounded tablespoonfuls 2 inches apart onto ungreased cookie sheets. Bake for 9 to 13 minutes or until edges are lightly browned. (Cookies will not brown; a slight imprint will remain when touched lightly in center.)

4. Just before serving, sprinkle with powdered sugar, if desired.

Nutrition Facts (1 cookie): Calories 70; Protein 1 g; Carbohydrate 10 g; Dietary Fiber 1 g; Fat 3 g; Cholesterol 10 mg; Sodium 55 mg

TIP Applesauce with a thicker consistency works best in this recipe.

Holiday Candy Cookies

This cookie boasts colorful, chocolate-coated candy pieces and vanilla milk chips. Use holiday paper or foil muffin pan liners for a festive touch.

Preparation time: 1 hour
Baking time: 15 minutes

[6 dozen cookies]

1⅓	cups firmly packed brown sugar
⅔	cup LAND O LAKES® Butter, softened
⅓	cup peanut butter
2	eggs
2	teaspoons vanilla
1	cup all-purpose flour
1	teaspoon baking powder
½	teaspoon baking soda
2½	cups quick-cooking oats
1	(10-ounce) package red and green chocolate candy-coated pieces
1	cup vanilla milk chips

1. Heat oven to 350°. Combine sugar, butter and peanut butter in large mixer bowl. Beat at medium speed, scraping bowl often, until well mixed (1 to 2 minutes). Add eggs and vanilla; beat until well mixed (1 to 2 minutes). Reduce speed to low; add flour, baking powder and baking soda. Beat until well mixed (1 to 2 minutes). Stir in oats, candy pieces and chips by hand.

2. Drop dough by heaping teaspoonfuls into paper-lined mini muffin pans. Bake for 15 to 17 minutes or until set and light golden brown. Let stand 2 minutes; remove from pans.

Nutrition Facts (1 cookie) Calories 90; Protein 1 g; Carbohydrate 11 g; Dietary Fiber 1 g; Fat 4 g; Cholesterol 10 mg; Sodium 50 mg

VARIATIONS

Giant Candy Cookies
Prepare recipe as directed *except* drop dough by ¼ cupfuls 3 inches apart onto ungreased cookie sheets. Flatten cookies to 3-inch diameter. Bake for 13 to 15 minutes or until light golden brown. Let stand 1 minute; remove from cookie sheets.
[1½ dozen giant cookies]

Traditional Candy Cookies
Prepare recipe as directed *except* drop dough by rounded tablespoonfuls 2 inches apart onto ungreased cookie sheets. Flatten cookies to 2-inch diameter. Bake for 12 to 14 minutes or until light golden brown. Let stand 1 minute; remove from cookie sheets.
[3 dozen (2½-inch) cookies]

TIP Paper liners for mini muffin pans vary considerably in size. The liners used for these cookies are 1-inch diameter and sometimes called petit four cups.

Lemon Doodles

Crisp on the outside and chewy on the inside, the lemon flavor adds a new twist to ever-popular snickerdoodles.

Preparation time: 45 minutes
Baking time: 7 minutes

[4 dozen cookies]

2½	cups all-purpose flour
1½	cups sugar
1	cup LAND O LAKES® Butter, softened
¾	cup flaked coconut
2	eggs
1	tablespoon lemon juice
1½	teaspoons cream of tartar
1	teaspoon baking soda
½	teaspoon grated lemon zest
¼	teaspoon salt

1. Heat oven to 400°. Combine all ingredients in large mixer bowl. Beat at low speed, scraping bowl often, until well mixed (2 to 4 minutes).

2. Drop dough by rounded teaspoonfuls 2 inches apart onto ungreased cookie sheets. Bake for 7 to 10 minutes or until edges are lightly browned.

Nutrition Facts (1 cookie): Calories 90; Protein 1 g; Carbohydrate 12 g; Dietary Fiber 0 g; Fat 5 g; Cholesterol 20 mg; Sodium 75 mg

Holiday Candy Cookies

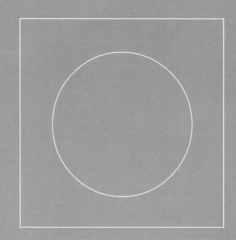

Simple Icebox

No matter how you cut it, these cookies are simple: just slice and bake. Keep a few batches of the dough in the freezer to bake for quick, sweet satisfaction. All icebox doughs will need to chill awhile before slicing and baking (hence their name), so plan on preparing them a day or two ahead, or tend to other kitchen tasks while you wait.

Chocolate Pinwheels

Technique

Most icebox cookie doughs are best when refrigerated overnight.

Use a thin-bladed, sharp knife when cutting the chilled dough, and wipe it occasionally with a clean paper towel.

To keep the roll from flattening on one side when you cut, turn it every few slices.
Once mixed, the dough can be refrigerated for up to a week. Simply wrap it securely in plastic food wrap, twisting the ends to protect the dough from drying out.

To freeze the dough, shape into a roll and place in a resealable plastic freezer bag before putting in freezer. To bake, remove the dough from the freezer and allow it to thaw in the refrigerator overnight or at room temperature until the dough is firm but easy to cut, about 30 minutes to one hour.

Chocolate Pinwheels

White and dark chocolate dough swirl into pretty pinwheels.

Preparation time: 40 minutes
Chilling time: 3 hours
Baking time: 7 minutes

[5 dozen cookies]

1	cup sugar
1/2	cup LAND O LAKES® Butter, softened
1	egg
2	teaspoons vanilla
2	(1-ounce) squares white baking bars, melted, cooled
1 2/3	cups all-purpose flour
1/2	teaspoon baking powder
1/4	teaspoon salt
1	(1-ounce) square unsweetened baking chocolate, melted, cooled

1. Combine sugar, butter, egg and vanilla in large mixer bowl. Beat at medium speed, scraping bowl often, until creamy (2 to 3 minutes). Reduce speed to low; add melted white baking bars. Beat until well mixed (about 1 minute). Add flour, baking powder and salt; continue beating until well mixed (1 to 2 minutes).

2. Remove *half* of dough. Add cooled melted chocolate to remaining dough in bowl. Beat until well mixed (about 1 minute). Shape each half of dough into 6x3-inch rectangle. Wrap in plastic food wrap. Refrigerate until firm (at least 1 hour).

3. Roll out white dough, on lightly floured waxed paper, to 15x7-inch rectangle. Repeat with chocolate dough. Place chocolate dough on top of white dough. Roll up, jelly-roll style, starting with 15-inch side. (For easier handling, roll can be cut in half.) Wrap roll in plastic food wrap. Refrigerate until firm (at least 2 hours).

4. *Heat oven to 375°.* Cut rolls into 1/4-inch slices with sharp knife. Place 2 inches apart on ungreased cookie sheets. Bake for 7 to 9 minutes or until edges are lightly browned. Cool completely.

Nutrition Facts (1 cookie): Calories 50; Protein 1 g; Carbohydrate 7 g; Dietary Fiber 0 g; Fat 3 g; Cholesterol 5 mg; Sodium 30 mg

TIP   When baking cookies it is best to place the cookie sheet on the center rack of an oven that's been preheated 10 to 15 minutes. Try not to bake more than one sheet at a time; the cookies will brown more evenly if they do not have to share oven space.

Butterscotch Crisps

Pecans and butterscotch chips are packed into this cookie, giving it a buttery crunch.

Preparation time: 45 minutes
Chilling time: 2 hours
Baking time: 5 minutes

[6 dozen cookies]

1	cup butterscotch-flavored baking chips
2¾	cups all-purpose flour
1	cup LAND O LAKES® Butter, softened
½	cup sugar
½	cup firmly packed brown sugar
1	egg
½	teaspoon baking soda
½	cup chopped pecans

1. Melt butterscotch chips in 1-quart saucepan over low heat, stirring constantly, until melted (3 to 5 minutes).

2. Place butterscotch mixture in large mixer bowl; add all remaining ingredients *except* pecans. Beat at low speed, scraping bowl often, until well mixed (1 to 2 minutes). Stir in pecans by hand.

3. Divide dough in half. Shape each half into 8x1½-inch roll. Wrap in plastic food wrap. Refrigerate until firm (at least 2 hours).

4. *Heat oven to 400°.* Cut rolls into ⅛-inch slices with sharp knife. Place 1 inch apart on ungreased cookie sheets. Bake for 5 to 7 minutes or until set. Cool 1 minute; remove from cookie sheets.

Nutrition Facts (1 cookie): Calories 75; Protein 1 g; Carbohydrate 9 g; Dietary Fiber 1 g; Fat 4 g; Cholesterol 12 mg; Sodium 39 mg

TIP Pecans are a high-fat nut that will turn rancid if stored at room temperature. Refrigerate shelled pecans for 6 to 9 months in an airtight, resealable container or freeze for up to two years. Always taste pecans, or any nut, before adding to your dough. If the nuts have a bitter or musty flavor, discard and buy a fresh supply.

[kitchen notes]

To make handling icebox cookie dough even easier, keep the following in mind: If your roll of dough becomes flattened in the refrigerator, simply roll to reshape before unwrapping.

Use a serrated knife to slice cookies; it will cut through fruit or nuts more efficiently.

For chewier cookies, slice dough into ¼-inch rounds instead of ⅛-inch. You may need to adjust baking time to be slightly longer.

Chocolate Almond Wafers

These elegant cookies are a hit at the dessert table.

Preparation time: 1 hour
Chilling time: 2 hours
Baking time: 9 minutes
Cooling time: 15 minutes

[8 dozen cookies]

DOUGH

1	cup sugar
¾	cup LAND O LAKES® Butter, softened
3	(1-ounce) squares unsweetened baking chocolate, melted
1	egg
1	teaspoon almond extract
1¼	cups all-purpose flour
1	teaspoon baking powder
½	teaspoon salt
½	cup blanched almonds, chopped

GLAZES

2	(1-ounce) squares bittersweet baking chocolate
2	(1-ounce) squares white baking bar
2	teaspoons shortening

1. Combine sugar, butter, melted chocolate, egg and almond extract in large mixer bowl. Beat at medium speed, scraping bowl often, until creamy (1 to 2 minutes). Reduce speed to low; add flour, baking powder and salt. Beat until well mixed (1 to 2 minutes). Stir in almonds by hand.

2. Divide dough in half. Shape each half on waxed paper into 12x1¼-inch roll. Wrap in waxed paper or plastic food wrap. Refrigerate until firm (2 hours or overnight).

3. *Heat oven to 350°.* Cut rolls into ¼-inch slices with sharp knife. Place 1 inch apart on ungreased cookie sheets. Bake for 9 to 11 minutes or until set. Cool completely.

4. Meanwhile, place bittersweet chocolate and 1 teaspoon shortening in small microwave-safe bowl. Place white baking bar and remaining shortening in another small microwave-safe bowl. Microwave on MEDIUM until melted (2 to 3 minutes). Drizzle cooled cookies with both glazes.

Nutrition Facts (1 cookie): Calories 45; Protein 1 g; Carbohydrate 4 g; Dietary Fiber 0 g; Fat 3 g; Cholesterol 5 mg; Sodium 30 mg

Mint Slices

This three-color, mint-flavored cookie is perfect for the holidays and other special occasions.

Preparation time: 1 hour 30 minutes
Chilling time: 3 hours
Baking time: 9 minutes

[11 dozen cookies]

1	cup sugar
1	cup LAND O LAKES® Butter, softened
1	egg
1	teaspoon peppermint extract
2⅓	cups all-purpose flour
¼	teaspoon baking powder
3	drops red food color
3	drops green food color

1. Combine sugar and butter in large mixer bowl. Beat at medium speed, scraping bowl often, until creamy (1 to 2 minutes). Add egg and peppermint extract. Continue beating until well mixed (1 to 2 minutes). Reduce speed to low; add flour and baking powder. Continue beating, scraping bowl often, until well mixed (1 to 2 minutes).

2. Divide dough into thirds. Add red food color to one-third. Add green food color to another third. Stir each until well mixed. Leave remaining dough white. Wrap dough in plastic food wrap; refrigerate until firm (at least 1 hour).

3. Divide each color of dough into thirds; shape each third into 12x½-inch rope on waxed paper. Gently press together 1 pink and 1 green rope. Add 1 white rope; gently press to form 1 clover leaf-shaped, multi-colored roll. Wrap each multi-colored roll in plastic food wrap; refrigerate until firm (at least 2 hours or overnight).

4. *Heat oven to 350°.* Cut rolls into ¼-inch slices with sharp knife. Place 1 inch apart on ungreased cookie sheets. Bake for 9 to 12 minutes or until edges are very lightly browned.

Nutrition Facts (1 cookie): Calories 25; Protein 0 g; Carbohydrate 3 g; Dietary Fiber 0 g; Fat 2 g; Cholesterol 5 mg; Sodium 15 mg

Chocolate Almond Wafers

Swedish Coconut Cookies

A Scandinavian heritage is the foundation for this buttery, tender cookie.

Preparation time: 1 hour 15 minutes
Chilling time: 2 hours
Baking time: 10 minutes

[8 dozen cookies]

$3\frac{1}{2}$ cups all-purpose flour
2   cups sugar
2   cups LAND O LAKES®
      Butter, softened
1   tablespoon baking powder
1   teaspoon baking soda
1   teaspoon vanilla
1   cup flaked coconut

1. Combine all ingredients *except* coconut in large mixer bowl. Beat at low speed, scraping bowl often, until well mixed (3 to 4 minutes). Stir in coconut by hand.

2. Divide dough in half; shape each half into 12x2-inch roll. Wrap each roll in plastic food wrap; refrigerate until firm (at least 2 hours).

3. *Heat oven to 350°.* Cut rolls into $\frac{1}{4}$-inch slices with sharp knife. Place 2 inches apart on ungreased cookie sheets. Bake for 10 to 14 minutes or until edges are lightly browned. Let stand 1 minute; remove from cookie sheets.

Nutrition Facts (1 cookie): Calories 70; Protein 1 g; Carbohydrate 8 g; Dietary Fiber 0 g; Fat 4 g; Cholesterol 10 mg; Sodium 70 mg

Chocolate Pecan Cookies

Finely chopped pecans ring the edge of these chocolate refrigerator cookies.

Preparation time: 1 hour
Chilling time: 4 hours
Baking time: 9 minutes

[$7\frac{1}{2}$ dozen cookies]

$1\frac{1}{2}$ cups sugar
1   cup LAND O LAKES®
      Butter, softened
2   eggs
2   teaspoons vanilla
4   (1-ounce) squares
      unsweetened baking
      chocolate, melted, cooled
$2\frac{3}{4}$ cups all-purpose flour
1   teaspoon baking powder
$\frac{1}{4}$ teaspoon salt
1   cup finely chopped pecans

1. Combine sugar and butter in large mixer bowl. Beat at medium speed, scraping bowl often, until creamy (1 to 2 minutes). Add eggs and vanilla; continue beating until well mixed (1 to 2 minutes).

2. Reduce speed to low; add chocolate. Beat until well mixed (1 minute). Add flour, baking powder and salt; continue beating, scraping bowl often, until well mixed (1 to 2 minutes). Cover; refrigerate until firm (at least 1 hour).

3. Divide dough into thirds. Shape each third into 8x1$\frac{3}{4}$-inch roll; roll in finely chopped pecans. Wrap in plastic food wrap. Refrigerate until firm (at least 3 hours).

4. *Heat oven to 350°.* Cut roll into $\frac{1}{4}$-inch slices with sharp knife. Place 1 inch apart on ungreased cookie sheets. Bake for 9 to 12 minutes or until set.

Nutrition Facts (1 cookie): Calories 60; Protein 1 g; Carbohydrate 7 g; Dietary Fiber 0 g; Fat 4 g; Cholesterol 10 mg; Sodium 35

TIP To chop nuts finely, you can use a small grinder or food processor fitted with a metal blade. Be careful not to process the nuts into a paste. Adding a small amount of flour (a teaspoon or less) to the nuts will help prevent them from clumping together.

Customize this recipe with dark or milk chocolate, and partner with a mug of hot cocoa to chase away the chill of a blustery day.

Chocolate Ribbons

Layers of dough are ribboned through delicate slices.

Preparation time: 30 minutes
Chilling time: 4 hours
Baking time: 8 minutes

[6 dozen cookies]

2½ cups all-purpose flour
1¼ cups sugar
1   cup LAND O LAKES®
     Butter, softened
1   egg
¼   teaspoon salt
2   teaspoons vanilla
1   (3-ounce) bar white chocolate,
     melted
3   (1-ounce) squares semi-sweet
     baking chocolate, melted

1. Combine all ingredients *except* white chocolate and semi-sweet chocolate in large mixer bowl. Beat at low speed, scraping bowl often, until well mixed (1 to 2 minutes).

2. Divide dough in half. To one half add melted white chocolate. Beat at low speed until well mixed (1 to 2 minutes). To second half add melted semi-sweet chocolate. Beat at low speed until well mixed (1 to 2 minutes).

3. Shape each half of dough into 5-inch square. Wrap in plastic food wrap. Refrigerate until firm (at least 2 hours).

4. Cut each 5-inch square into quarters (forming 2½-inch squares). Roll out each quarter to 10x4-inch rectangle on lightly floured piece of waxed paper. Wrap each rectangle in plastic food wrap. Refrigerate until firm (at least 1 hour).

5. Unwrap rectangles of dough. Stack rectangles, alternating colors and brushing dough lightly with water; press each layer lightly to seal. Cover with plastic food wrap. Refrigerate until firm (at least 1 hour).

6. *Heat oven to 375°.* Unwrap dough. Trim off ends of dough with sharp knife to make even. Cut into ¼-inch slices with sharp knife; cut each cookie slice in half. Place on ungreased cookie sheets using spatula.

7. Bake for 8 to 10 minutes or until edges are very lightly browned. (DO NOT OVER-BAKE.) Let stand 1 minute; remove from cookie sheets.

Nutrition Facts (1 cookie): Calories 70; Protein 1 g; Carbohydrate 8 g; Dietary Fibe 0 g; Fat 3 g; Cholesterol 10 mg; Sodium 35 mg

Citrus Slice 'N Bake Cookies

The flavors of orange and lemon shine in these delicate butter cookies.

Preparation time: 1 hour 15 minutes
Chilling time: 2 hours
Baking time: 7 minutes

[4 dozen cookies]

COOKIE

2   cups all-purpose flour
1 1/4   cups powdered sugar
3/4   cup LAND O LAKES® Butter, softened
1   egg
1   teaspoon baking powder
1   teaspoon grated orange zest
2   teaspoons lemon extract
1/2   teaspoon salt
1/4   teaspoon baking soda

SUGAR

1/4   cup sugar
4   drops yellow food color
2   drops red food color
2   tablespoons LAND O LAKES® Butter, melted

1. Combine all cookie ingredients in large mixer bowl. Beat at low speed, scraping bowl often, until well mixed (2 to 3 minutes).

2. Divide dough in half. Shape each half into 6x1 1/2-inch roll. Wrap in plastic food wrap. Refrigerate until firm (at least 2 hours).

3. Meanwhile, combine sugar and yellow food color in jar with tight-fitting lid. Cover; shake until well blended (1 to 2 minutes). Remove 2 tablespoons yellow sugar; add red food color to remaining sugar. Cover; shake until well blended (1 to 2 minutes).

4. *Heat oven to 375°.* Cut rolls in half lengthwise with sharp knife; brush with melted butter. Roll *2 halves* in yellow sugar and *2 halves* in orange sugar. Cut rolls into 1/4-inch slices with sharp knife. Place 1 inch apart on ungreased cookie sheets. Bake for 7 to 10 minutes or until edges are lightly browned.

Nutrition Facts (1 cookie): Calories 60; Protein 1 g; Carbohydrate 8 g; Dietary Fiber 0 g; Fat 4 g; Cholesterol 15 mg; Sodium 70 mg

Black Walnut Icebox Cookies

Black walnuts give this brown sugar cookie its nutty, rich flavor.

Preparation time: 45 minutes
Chilling time: 2 hours
Baking time: 6 minutes

[8 dozen cookies]

3 1/2   cups all-purpose flour
2   cups firmly packed brown sugar
1   cup LAND O LAKES® Butter, softened
2   eggs
1 1/2   teaspoons baking soda
1/2   teaspoon salt
1/2   teaspoon vanilla
1/2   cup chopped black walnuts *or* walnuts

1. Combine all ingredients *except* walnuts in large mixer bowl. Beat at low speed, scraping bowl often, until well mixed (3 to 4 minutes). Stir in walnuts by hand.

2. Divide dough in half. Shape each half on lightly floured surface into 10x1 1/2-inch roll. Wrap in plastic food wrap. Refrigerate until firm (at least 2 hours).

3. *Heat oven to 400°.* Cut rolls into 1/8-inch slices with sharp knife. Place 1 inch apart on ungreased cookie sheets. Bake for 6 to 8 minutes or until lightly browned.

Nutrition Facts (1 cookie): Calories 60; Protein 1 g; Carbohydrate 8 g; Dietary Fiber 0 g; Fat 2 g; Cholesterol 10 mg; Sodium 50 mg

TIP Black walnuts have a slightly bitter, strong taste and are more flavorful than English walnuts. Their hard shell makes them tough to crack, but they partner nicely with sweets.

Citrus Slice 'N Bake Cookies

Cinnamon Coffee Cookies

Coffee, pecans and cinnamon flavor these easy, glazed slice-and-bake cookies.

Preparation time: 1 hour 30 minutes
Chilling time: 1 hour
Baking time: 6 minutes

[8 dozen cookies]

COOKIE

1	cup firmly packed brown sugar
¾	cup LAND O LAKES® Butter, softened
¼	cup orange juice
1	tablespoon grated orange zest
2¾	cups all-purpose flour
½	cup finely chopped pecans
1	tablespoon instant espresso coffee powder
1¾	teaspoons baking powder
1	teaspoon ground cinnamon
½	teaspoon salt

GLAZE

1½	cups powdered sugar
¾	teaspoon instant espresso coffee powder
3-4	tablespoons orange juice
96	chocolate-covered coffee beans *or* chocolate-dipped pecans, if desired

1. Combine brown sugar and butter in large mixer bowl. Beat at medium speed, scraping bowl often, until creamy (1 to 2 minutes). Add ¼ cup orange juice and orange zest. Continue beating until well mixed (1 minute).

2. Reduce speed to low; add all remaining cookie ingredients. Beat until well mixed (1 to 2 minutes).

3. Divide dough in half. Shape each half into 15x1¼-inch roll. Wrap in plastic food wrap. Refrigerate until firm (at least 1 hour).

4. *Heat oven to 375°.* Cut rolls into ¼-inch slices with sharp knife. Place 1 inch apart on lightly greased cookie sheets. Flatten slightly with bottom of glass. Bake for 6 to 8 minutes or until edges are lightly browned.

5. Meanwhile, combine powdered sugar and ¾ teaspoon espresso coffee powder in small bowl. Gradually stir in enough orange juice for desired glazing consistency. Spoon about *¼ teaspoon* glaze over each warm cookie; lightly press chocolate-covered coffee bean on top of each cookie.

Nutrition Facts (1 cookie): Calories 45; Protein 1 g; Carbohydrate 7 g; Dietary Fiber 0 g; Fat 2 g; Cholesterol 5 mg; Sodium 30 mg

Scandinavian Ginger Snaps

These thin, crisp ginger cookies are a holiday tradition in Norway.

Preparation time: 50 minutes
Chilling time: 4 hours
Baking time: 7 minutes

[5 dozen cookies]

2⅓	cups all-purpose flour
1½	teaspoons baking soda
1	teaspoon baking powder
1	teaspoon ground cinnamon
1	teaspoon ground ginger
½	teaspoon salt
½	teaspoon ground cloves
1	cup sugar
¾	cup LAND O LAKES® Butter
1	egg
¼	cup dark molasses

1. Combine flour, baking soda, baking powder, cinnamon, ginger, salt and cloves in medium bowl; set aside.

2. Combine sugar and butter in large mixer bowl. Beat at medium speed, scraping bowl often, until creamy (1 to 2 minutes). Add egg and molasses. Continue beating until well mixed (1 to 2 minutes). Reduce speed to low; add flour mixture. Beat, scraping bowl often, until well mixed (1 to 2 minutes).

3. Divide dough in half. Shape each half into 9x1½-inch roll on waxed paper. Wrap in plastic food wrap. Refrigerate until firm (at least 4 hours).

4. *Heat oven to 375°.* Cut rolls into ¼-inch slices with sharp knife. Place 2 inches apart on ungreased cookie sheets. Bake for 7 to 10 minutes or until set.

Nutrition Facts (1 cookie): Calories 60; Protein 1 g; Carbohydrate 8 g; Dietary Fiber 0 g; Fat 3 g; Cholesterol 10 mg; Sodium 70 mg

Orange Cornmeal Crisps

Made of cornmeal with a hint of orange, these cookies are a tasty, healthy afternoon snack that's not overly sweet.

Preparation time: 1 hour 20 minutes
Chilling time: 1 hour
Baking time: 8 minutes

[7 dozen cookies]

1	cup sugar
1	cup LAND O LAKES® Butter, softened
1	egg
2	cups all-purpose flour
¾	cup cornmeal
1	tablespoon grated orange zest
2	teaspoons baking powder
½	teaspoon ground nutmeg

1. Combine sugar, butter and egg in large mixer bowl. Beat at medium speed, scraping bowl often, until creamy (1 to 2 minutes). Reduce speed to low; add all remaining ingredients. Beat until well mixed (1 to 2 minutes).

2. Divide dough in half. Shape each half into 12x1½ x1½-inch square roll. Wrap in plastic food wrap. Refrigerate until firm (at least 1 hour).

3. *Heat oven to 375°.* Cut rolls into ¼-inch slices with sharp knife. Place 1 inch apart on ungreased cookie sheets. Imprint 3 tines at each corner of cookies with fork to make design. Bake for 8 to 12 minutes or until edges are lightly browned.

Nutrition Facts (1 cookie): Calories 40; Protein 1 g; Carbohydrate 6 g; Dietary Fiber 0 g; Fat 2 g; Cholesterol 10 mg; Sodium 30 mg

TIP Cornmeal is simply dried corn kernels that have been ground, typically with steel or stone rollers. Cornmeal comes in a variety of colors, including yellow, white or blue. While blue has the strongest flavor and is sometimes used in muffins or bread, yellow or white cornmeal is preferred for this recipe. Stored in an airtight container in a cool, dry place, cornmeal will keep almost indefinitely.

[kitchen notes]

The zest or outer peel of citrus fruits contains aromatic and highly flavorful oils that add both color and flavor to many recipes. To properly "zest" an orange, lemon or lime, use a zester, which has five tiny round holes on its cutting surface, or a small grater. Grate only down to the white membrane or pith, which has a bitter flavor.

Oatmeal Gumdrop Cookies

This slice-and-bake oatmeal cookie will be your family's favorite.

Preparation time: 50 minutes
Chilling time: 2 hours
Baking time: 10 minutes

[4 dozen cookies]

1	cup sugar
½	cup LAND O LAKES® Butter, softened
¼	cup firmly packed brown sugar
2	eggs
1	teaspoon vanilla
2	cups all-purpose flour
1	cup quick-cooking oats
1	teaspoon baking soda
½	teaspoon salt
1	cup chopped gumdrops

1. Combine sugar, butter and brown sugar in large mixer bowl. Beat at medium speed, scraping bowl often, until creamy (1 to 2 minutes). Add eggs and vanilla; continue beating until well mixed (1 minute). Reduce speed to low; add flour, oats, baking soda and salt. Beat until well mixed (1 to 2 minutes).

2. Stir in gumdrops by hand. Shape dough into two 9x1½-inch rolls. Wrap in waxed paper; refrigerate until firm (at least 2 hours).

3. *Heat oven to 350°.* Cut rolls into ⅜-inch slices, using serrated knife. Place 1 inch apart on lightly greased cookie sheets. Bake for 10 to 12 minutes or until lightly browned and set. Immediately remove from cookie sheets. Cool completely.

Nutrition Facts (1 cookie): Calories 80; Protein 1 g; Carbohydrate 14 g; Dietary Fiber 0 g; Fat 2.5 g; Cholesterol 15 mg; Sodium 75 mg

Tip Carefully cut gumdrops into small pieces using kitchen scissors. Dip the blades into water to prevent sticking.

Date Pinwheels

This is a favorite from our test kitchens, originating two generations ago.

Preparation time: 1 hour 20 minutes
Cooling time: 30 minutes
Chilling time: 2 hours
Baking time: 9 minutes

[6 dozen cookies]

FILLING

½	cup water
¼	cup sugar
1	(8-ounce) package chopped dates
1	teaspoon lemon juice

DOUGH

¾	cup firmly packed brown sugar
½	cup LAND O LAKES® Butter, softened
1	egg
1	teaspoon vanilla
1¾	cups all-purpose flour
1	teaspoon baking powder
¼	teaspoon salt

1. Combine all filling ingredients in 1-quart saucepan. Cook over medium-high heat, stirring occasionally, until mixture thickens and comes to a boil (3 to 5 minutes). Cool to room temperature (30 minutes).

2. Combine brown sugar, butter, egg and vanilla in large mixer bowl. Beat at medium speed, scraping bowl often, until creamy (1 to 2 minutes). Reduce speed to low; add flour, baking powder and salt. Beat until well mixed (1 to 2 minutes).

3. Divide dough in half. Roll out half of dough, on well-floured surface, to 12x8-inch rectangle. Spread half of filling to within ½ inch of edges. Roll up, jelly-roll style, starting with 12-inch side. Pinch edges to seal. Wrap rolls in plastic food wrap. Refrigerate until firm (at least 2 hours).

4. *Heat oven to 350°.* Cut rolls into ¼-inch slices with sharp knife. Place on lightly greased cookie sheets. Bake for 9 to 12 minutes or until edges begin to brown.

Nutrition Facts (1 cookie): Calories 45; Protein 0 g; Carbohydrate 8 g; Dietary Fiber 0 g; Fat 1.5 g; Cholesterol 5 mg; Sodium 30 mg

Oatmeal Gumdrop Cookies

Cherry Pecan Cookies

*This cookie makes a colorful
addition to the holiday
cookie platter.*

Preparation time: 2 hours
Chilling time: 4 hours
Baking time: 11 minutes

[10 dozen cookies]

1	cup LAND O LAKES® Butter, softened
½	cup sugar
½	cup powdered sugar
1	egg
1	teaspoon vanilla
2¼	cups all-purpose flour
1½	cups red *and/or* green candied cherries, halved
1	tablespoon all-purpose flour
1	cup coarsely chopped pecans

1. Combine butter, sugars, egg
and vanilla in large mixer bowl.
Beat at medium speed, scraping
bowl often, until creamy (2 to 3
minutes). Reduce speed to low;
add 2¼ cups flour. Beat until
well mixed (1 to 2 minutes).

2. Combine cherries and 1 tablespoon
flour in small bowl; toss to coat.
Stir cherry mixture and pecans
into dough by hand; mix well.
Cover; refrigerate until firm
(1 to 2 hours).

3. Shape dough into three 1-inch
diameter rolls on lightly floured
waxed paper; wrap in plastic
food wrap. Refrigerate until
firm (3 hours or overnight).

4. *Heat oven to 350°.* Cut rolls into
¼-inch slices with sharp knife. Place
1 inch apart on ungreased cookie
sheets. Bake for 11 to 13 minutes or
until edges are lightly browned.

Nutrition Facts (1 cookie): Calories 40; Protein 1 g;
Carbohydrate 5 g; Dietary Fiber 0 g; Fat 2 g;
Cholesterol 5 mg; Sodium 25 mg

Sesame Crisps

*This crisp wafer cookie is
reminiscent of a benne wafer.*

Preparation time: 1 hour
Chilling time: 2 hours
Baking time: 12 minutes

[4 dozen cookies]

1	cup LAND O LAKES® Butter, softened
⅔	cup sugar
1½	cups all-purpose flour
1	cup shredded coconut
½	cup sesame seed
¼	cup finely chopped almonds

1. Combine butter and sugar in
large mixer bowl. Beat at medium
speed until creamy. Reduce speed
to low; add flour. Beat until well
mixed (1 to 2 minutes). Stir in
coconut, sesame seeds and
almonds by hand.

2. Divide dough into thirds. On
waxed paper, shape each third into
4x1-inch roll. Wrap in plastic food
wrap; refrigerate until firm
(2 hours or overnight).

3. *Heat oven to 325°.* Cut rolls into
¼-inch slices with sharp knife. Place
1 inch apart on ungreased cookie
sheets. Bake for 12 to 17 minutes
or until edges are lightly browned.

Nutrition Facts (1 cookie): Calories 80; Protein 1 g;
Carbohydrate 7 g; Dietary Fiber 0 g; Fat 6 g;
Cholesterol 10 mg; Sodium 45 mg

TIP Sesame seed is the first
recorded seasoning, dating to
3000 B.C. Boasting a mildly
sweet, nutty flavor, sesame seed
complements both sweet and
savory dishes and is popular in
African, Indian and oriental
cuisines. Because of its high oil
content, sesame seed can turn
rancid quickly. Store in a cool,
dry place for up to 3 months, or
up to 6 months in the refrigerator.

Cherry Pecan Cookies

Royal Icing

Royal icing hardens as it dries and is ideal for piping decorations on cooled cookies.

Preparation time: 10 minutes

[¾ cup]

1¼	cups sifted powdered sugar
1	tablespoon meringue powder
2	tablespoons warm water
¼	teaspoon cream of tartar

1. Combine all ingredients in large mixer bowl. Beat at low speed until moistened. Increase speed to medium. Beat until stiff and glossy (2 to 4 minutes). Add additional tablespoon hot water if too stiff.

2. Cover bowl with damp paper towel until ready to use or cover with plastic food wrap and refrigerate for up to 2 weeks. To restore texture, allow icing to reach room temperature, then re-beat.

Nutrition Facts (1 tablespoon): Calories 50; Protein 0 g; Carbohydrate 13 g; Dietary Fiber 0 g; Fat 0 g; Cholesterol 0 mg; Sodium 5 mg

TIP Meringue powder is available at large supermarkets and specialty cooking shops.

Powdered Sugar Glaze

This frosting hardens on standing and gives cookies a glazed surface for decorating.

Preparation time: 10 minutes

[1 cup]

2½	cups powdered sugar
2	tablespoons water
1	tablespoon LAND O LAKES® Butter, softened
1	tablespoon light corn syrup
½	teaspoon almond extract *or* vanilla, if desired

Food color, if desired

1. Combine powdered sugar, water, butter, corn syrup, and vanilla in small mixer bowl; mix until powdered sugar is moistened. Beat at medium speed until smooth, adding additional water if necessary to achieve desired spreading consistency. Tint with food color, if desired.

2. Frost cooled cookies. Let stand until hardened (6 hours or overnight).

Nutrition Facts (1 tablespoon): Calories 80; Protein 0 g; Carbohydrate 20 g; Dietary Fiber 0 g; Fat .5 g; Cholesterol 0 mg; Sodium 10 mg

Creamy Butter Frosting

This creamy frosting is great for decorating cookies and bars. If desired, it can be tinted with food coloring.

Preparation time: 10 minutes

[2¼ cups]

4	cups powdered sugar
½	cup LAND O LAKES® Butter, softened
2	teaspoons vanilla
3-4	tablespoons milk

Food color, if desired

1. Combine powdered sugar, butter and vanilla in small mixer bowl. Beat at low speed, gradually adding milk and scraping bowl often, until desired spreading consistency. Add food color, if desired. Decorate cooled cookies or bars. Cover; store refrigerated.

Nutrition Facts (1 tablespoon): Calories 80; Protein 0 g; Carbohydrate 13 g; Dietary Fiber 0 g; Fat 2.5 g; Cholesterol 5 mg; Sodium 25 mg

TIP To use frosting later, bring to room temperature; mix well.

Best Buttercream Frosting

This creamy butter frosting makes a perfect base for varied flavorings.

Preparation time: 10 minutes

[3 cups]

¾	cup LAND O LAKES® Butter, softened
6	cups powdered sugar
⅛	teaspoon salt
⅓	cup whipping cream
1	teaspoon vanilla
2	tablespoons light corn syrup

1. Beat butter in large mixer bowl at medium speed until creamy (1 to 2 minutes).

2. Gradually add powdered sugar and salt alternately with whipping cream and vanilla, scraping bowl often, until well blended. Beat in corn syrup until well mixed.

Nutrition Facts (1 tablespoon): Calories 90; Protein 0 g; Carbohydrate 16 g; Dietary Fiber 0 g; Fat 3.5 g; Cholesterol 10 mg; Sodium 35 mg

VARIATIONS

Chocolate Frosting
Add 2 to 3 squares melted unsweetened baking chocolate.

Lemon or Orange Frosting
Stir in 1 tablespoon grated lemon *or* orange zest.

Creamy Coconut Frosting
Stir in 1½ teaspoons coconut extract *or* flavoring.

[kitchen notes]

Homemade cookies are a welcome gift. Mail them to family and friends using the following guidelines, and they're sure to arrive looking as attractive as they are delicious. Keep in mind that bars, drop cookies and fruit cookies tend to "travel better" than delicate, wafer-like cookies.

Use a heavy cardboard box as a mailing container, and line it with aluminum foil or plastic wrap.

Wrap small packages of cookies of the same size and variety in aluminum foil, resealable plastic food bags or plastic wrap. Set the heaviest bundles of cookies at the bottom of the resealable container, and use crumpled paper towels to separate layers of cookie packages (try not to layer the bundles more than three rows deep).

Tape the resealable container closed with strong tape before placing it in the mailing container.

Address the mailing container, then write "Perishable Food" and "Fragile" on the package to ensure careful handling.

Hand-Formed Classics

Many of America's cookie traditions are expressed through simple handmade techniques: rich, tiny tea cakes, tempting spritz, or whimsical teddy bears. Visually impressive and always delicious, these and other hand-formed classics are cookies that will be warmly remembered for years.

Stamped Ginger Cookies

Technique

Many of these doughs tend to become sticky when over-handled. To firm up soft dough, simply cover and place in the refrigerator for 30 minutes, then proceed with the recipe.

These cookies may require a little more time to prepare. If you find yourself running short on time and need to clean up before you've finished baking every batch, tightly cover the remaining dough with plastic wrap and store in the refrigerator.

Shaped cookies tend to be more delicate, and therefore are best stored in airtight containers, layered between sheets of waxed paper.

Stamped Ginger Cookies

These tender butter cookies are seasoned with crystallized ginger. Use a favorite cookie stamp or mold for a decorative finish.

Preparation time: 35 minutes
Baking time: 12 minutes

[3½ dozen cookies]

1	cup LAND O LAKES® Butter, softened
⅔	cup powdered sugar
1	teaspoon vanilla
2	cups all-purpose flour
½	teaspoon ground ginger
¼	teaspoon salt
¼	cup finely chopped crystallized ginger

1. Heat oven to 325°. Combine butter, powdered sugar and vanilla in large mixer bowl. Beat at medium speed, scraping bowl often, until creamy (1 to 2 minutes). Reduce speed to low; add flour, ground ginger and salt. Beat until well mixed (1 minute). Stir in crystallized ginger by hand.

2. Shape dough into 1-inch balls. Place 2 inches apart on ungreased cookie sheets. With prepared 2-inch cookie stamp, flatten balls to ¼ inch. Bake for 12 to 15 minutes or until edges just begin to brown. Let stand 2 to 3 minutes; remove from cookie sheets.

Nutrition Facts (1 cookie): Calories 70; Protein 1 g; Carbohydrate 7 g; Dietary Fiber 0 g; Fat 4.5 g; Cholesterol 10 mg; Sodium 60 mg

TIP Crystallized ginger can be chopped in a mini food processor. Add 1 teaspoon sugar to ginger while chopping.

VARIATION *Omit ground and crystallized ginger.* Add 2 to 3 drops food color to tint dough; add ½ teaspoon almond or peppermint extract. Dough tinted with food color often makes the design more distinct.

TIP Cookie stamps date back to a time when cookies were embossed with animals, saints or religious symbols important to celebrations and feasts. To prevent dough from sticking to stamps or molds, lightly spray with no stick cooking spray.

Hazelnut Rounds

Hazelnuts, also called filberts, are sweet and rich, giving depth and texture to this fragile butter cookie.

Preparation time: 50 minutes
Chilling time: 1 hour
Baking time: 13 minutes

[4 dozen cookies]

1	cup sugar
1	cup LAND O LAKES® Butter, softened
1	egg
1	teaspoon vanilla
2	cups all-purpose flour
½	teaspoon baking soda
¼	teaspoon salt
1	(2½-ounce) package (½ cup) hazelnuts *or* filberts, finely chopped

1. Combine sugar and butter in large mixer bowl. Beat at medium speed, scraping bowl often, until creamy (1 to 2 minutes). Add egg and vanilla. Continue beating until well mixed (1 minute). Reduce speed to low; add flour, baking soda and salt. Beat until well mixed (1 to 2 minutes). Cover; refrigerate until firm (at least 1 hour).

2. *Heat oven to 350°.* Shape dough into 1-inch balls; roll in hazelnuts. Place 2 inches apart on ungreased cookie sheets. Bake for 13 to 16 minutes or until edges are lightly browned.

Nutrition Facts (1 cookie): Calories 80; Protein 1 g; Carbohydrate 8 g; Dietary Fiber 0 g; Fat 5 g; Cholesterol 15 mg; Sodium 60 mg

TIP If desired, melt ½ cup semi-sweet real chocolate chips and 1 teaspoon shortening in 1-quart saucepan over low heat until smooth. Drizzle chocolate mixture over cookies.

[kitchen notes]

Hazelnuts have a bitter brown skin that is best removed, usually by roasting.
Place the nuts on a small baking sheet and place in a preheated 400° oven for about
10 minutes, or until the skins begin to turn dark brown and crack. To remove the
skins, roll hazelnuts in a clean dish towel, rubbing off the skins.

Chocolate Chip Thumbprints

Bursting with mini chocolate chips, this traditional cookie features a glossy chocolate center.

Preparation time: 40 minutes
Baking time: 10 minutes
Cooling time: 30 minutes

[2 dozen cookies]

COOKIE
½   cup firmly packed brown sugar
½   cup LAND O LAKES® Butter, softened
1   teaspoon vanilla
½   teaspoon salt
1½ cups all-purpose flour
¼   cup mini-semi-sweet real chocolate chips
¼   cup milk

Powdered sugar

FILLING
¾   cup mini semi-sweet real chocolate chips
1   tablespoon shortening
2   tablespoons light corn syrup
1   teaspoon water
1   teaspoon vanilla

1. Heat oven to 375°. Combine brown sugar, butter, 1 teaspoon vanilla and salt in large mixer bowl. Beat at medium speed, scraping bowl often, until well mixed (1 to 2 minutes). Reduce speed to low; add flour, ¼ cup chocolate chips and milk. Beat until well mixed (1 to 2 minutes).

2. Shape dough into 1-inch balls. Place 1 inch apart on ungreased cookie sheets. Make indentation in center of each cookie with thumb.

3. Bake for 10 to 12 minutes or until lightly browned. (If necessary, make indentation in top of cookie again.) Cool completely. Sprinkle cookies with powdered sugar.

4. Melt ¾ cup chocolate chips and shortening in 1-quart saucepan over low heat, stirring occasionally, until smooth (1 to 2 minutes). Cool slightly. Stir in corn syrup, water and vanilla. Spoon about *1 teaspoon* filling into each cookie indentation.

Nutrition Facts (1 cookie): Calories 130; Protein 1 g; Carbohydrate 16 g; Dietary Fiber 1 g; Fat 7 g; Cholesterol 10 mg; Sodium 90 mg

Snickerdoodles

Simply a nineteenth-century nonsense word for a quickly made confection, "Snickerdoodle" has come to mean a coffee-break or after-school treat.

Preparation time: 45 minutes
Baking time: 8 minutes

[4 dozen cookies]

COOKIE
2¾ cups all-purpose flour
1½ cups sugar
1   cup LAND O LAKES® Butter, softened
2   eggs
2   teaspoons cream of tartar
1   teaspoon baking soda
1   teaspoon vanilla
¼   teaspoon salt

SUGAR MIXTURE
3   tablespoons sugar
1½ teaspoons ground cinnamon

1. Heat oven to 400°. Combine all cookie ingredients in large mixer bowl. Beat at low speed, scraping bowl often, until well mixed (2 to 4 minutes).

2. Stir together 3 tablespoons sugar and cinnamon in small bowl. Shape rounded teaspoonfuls of dough into 1-inch balls; roll in sugar-cinnamon mixture. Place 2 inches apart on ungreased cookie sheets. Bake for 8 to 10 minutes or until edges are lightly browned.

Nutrition Facts (1 cookie): Calories 90; Protein 1 g; Carbohydrate 13 g; Dietary Fiber 0 g; Fat 4 g; Cholesterol 20 mg; Sodium 80 mg

Chocolate Chip Thumbprints

Chocolate Pixies

Prepare the dough ahead and refrigerate, then bake these chocolate cookies the next day.

Preparation time: 45 minutes
Cooling time: 30 minutes
Chilling time: 2 hours
Baking time: 12 minutes

[4 dozen cookies]

¼   cup LAND O LAKES® Butter
4   (1-ounce) squares
     unsweetened baking chocolate
2   cups all-purpose flour
2   cups sugar
4   eggs
2   teaspoons baking powder
½   teaspoon salt
½   cup chopped walnuts
     or pecans

     Powdered sugar

1. Melt butter and chocolate in 1-quart saucepan over low heat, stirring occasionally, until smooth (8 to 10 minutes). Cool completely (30 minutes).

2. Combine melted chocolate mixture, *1 cup* flour, sugar, eggs, baking powder and salt in large mixer bowl. Beat at medium speed, scraping bowl often, until well mixed (2 to 3 minutes). Stir in remaining flour and nuts by hand. Cover; refrigerate until firm (at least 2 hours).

3. *Heat oven to 300°.* Shape rounded teaspoonfuls of dough into 1-inch balls; roll in powdered sugar. Place 2 inches apart on greased cookie sheets. Bake for 12 to 15 minutes or until set.

Nutrition Facts (1 cookie): Calories 90; Protein 2 g; Carbohydrate 13 g; Dietary Fiber 0 g; Fat 3 g; Cholesterol   20 mg; Sodium 50 mg

Java Tea Cakes

Coffee, cinnamon and butter create a luscious cookie recipe inspired by the Old South.

Preparation time: 45 minutes
Baking time: 15 minutes
Cooling time: 15 minutes

[3½ dozen cookies]

COOKIE
2   cups all-purpose flour
1   cup LAND O LAKES®
     Butter, softened
⅓   cup sugar
1   teaspoon instant coffee
     granules
½   teaspoon ground cinnamon
¼   teaspoon salt
1   cup finely chopped pecans

GLAZE
¼-½ teaspoon instant
     coffee granules
1   tablespoon milk
1   cup powdered sugar
1   teaspoon LAND O LAKES®
     Butter, softened

1. Heat oven to 350°. Combine all cookie ingredients *except* pecans in large mixer bowl. Beat at low speed, scraping bowl often, until well mixed (1 to 2 minutes). Stir in pecans by hand.

2. Shape rounded teaspoonfuls of dough into 1-inch balls. Place 2 inches apart on ungreased cookie sheets. Bake for 15 to 20 minutes or until edges are lightly browned. Cool completely.

3. Stir together ¼ to ½ teaspoon coffee granules and milk in small bowl with wire whisk until granules dissolve. Stir in powdered sugar and 1 teaspoon butter until smooth. If thinner glaze is desired, stir in additional milk, ½ teaspoon at a time. Dip tops of cookies in glaze.

Nutrition Facts (1 cookie): Calories 100; Protein 1 g; Carbohydrate 9 g; Dietary Fiber 0 g; Fat 6 g; Cholesterol 10 mg; Sodium 60 mg

TIP If desired, cookies can be rolled in powdered sugar rather than glazed.

TIP Use instant espresso granules for a stronger coffee flavor.

The quintessential autumn cookie, these treats boast subtle notes of ginger, cinnamon and clove for the perfect balance of sweetness and spice.

Chewy Molasses Crinkles

These chewy cookies gain a touch of crispness from a light sugar glaze formed while they bake.

Preparation time: 45 minutes
Chilling time: 30 minutes
Baking time: 10 minutes

[4 dozen cookies]

1	cup firmly packed brown sugar
¾	cup LAND O LAKES® Butter, softened
⅓	cup molasses
1	egg
2¼	cups all-purpose flour
2	teaspoons baking soda
1	teaspoon ground cinnamon
¾	teaspoon ground ginger
½	teaspoon ground cloves
¼	teaspoon salt
	Water
¼	cup sugar

1. Combine brown sugar and butter in large mixer bowl. Beat at medium speed, scraping bowl often, until creamy (2 to 3 minutes). Add molasses and egg; continue beating until well mixed (1 to 2 minutes). Reduce speed to low; add flour, baking soda, cinnamon, ginger, cloves and salt. Beat until well mixed (1 to 2 minutes). Cover; refrigerate 30 minutes.

2. *Heat oven to 350°.* Shape dough into 1-inch balls. Dip top of each ball into water, then in sugar. Place 2 inches apart on ungreased cookie sheets. Bake for 10 to 12 minutes or until set and lightly browned. Cool completely.

Nutrition Facts (1 cookie): Calories 80; Protein 1 g; Carbohydrate 12 g; Dietary Fiber 0 g; Fat 3 g; Cholesterol 10 mg; Sodium 95 mg

TIP Cookies can also be rolled in sugar without dipping in water first. The cookie will have a slightly less crackled appearance.

Mocha Toffee Crescents

These simply shaped cookies pair the richness of coffee and toffee.

Preparation time: 45 minutes
Baking time: 13 minutes

[3½ dozen cookies]

1	teaspoon instant espresso granules
1	tablespoon warm water
1	cup LAND O LAKES® Butter, softened
⅔	cup powdered sugar
2	cups all-purpose flour
¼	teaspoon salt
½	cup milk chocolate English toffee bits

1. Heat oven to 325°. Dissolve espresso granules in warm water in small bowl.

2. Combine espresso mixture, butter and powdered sugar in large mixer bowl. Beat at medium speed, scraping bowl often, until creamy (1 to 2 minutes). Reduce speed to low; add flour and salt. Beat until well mixed (1 to 2 minutes). Stir in toffee bits by hand.

3. Shape heaping teaspoonfuls of dough into crescents. Place 1 inch apart on ungreased cookie sheets. Bake for 13 to 17 minutes or until set but not brown. Let stand 1 minute; remove from cookie sheets.

Nutrition Facts (1 cookie): Calories 80; Protein 1 g; Carbohydrate 8 g; Dietary Fiber 0 g; Fat 5 g; Cholesterol 15 mg; Sodium 60 mg

TIP Cookies can be rolled in powdered sugar when warm or cool, or dip ends in mixture of melted ½ cup semi-sweet real chocolate chips and 2 teaspoons shortening.

TIP Cookies can also be shaped into 2½-inch logs or 1-inch balls. Bake as directed.

Rum-Glazed Shortbread Cookies

Sophisticated and pretty, these make tasteful additions to the party tray.

Preparation time: 40 minutes
Baking time: 13 minutes
Cooling time: 15 minutes

[3 dozen cookies]

COOKIE

1	cup LAND O LAKES® Butter, softened
½	cup powdered sugar
1	teaspoon vanilla
1¾	cups all-purpose flour

GLAZE

1	cup powdered sugar
1	tablespoon LAND O LAKES® Butter, softened
½	teaspoon rum extract
1-2	tablespoons hot water
½	cup chopped pecans

1. Heat oven to 350°. Combine all cookie ingredients in large mixer bowl. Beat at low speed, scraping bowl often, until well mixed (3 to 4 minutes).

2. Shape dough into ½-inch balls. Place 1 inch apart on ungreased cookie sheet; flatten balls with bottom of glass. Bake for 13 to 16 minutes or until lightly browned. Cool completely.

3. Stir together powdered sugar, butter, rum extract and enough hot water for desired glazing consistency in small bowl. Drizzle over cookies; sprinkle with chopped pecans.

Nutrition Facts (1 cookie): Calories 100; Protein 1 g; Carbohydrate 10 g; Dietary Fiber 0 g; Fat 7 g; Cholesterol 15 mg; Sodium 55 mg

TIP Be sure baking sheets have had a chance to cool before filling with a new batch of unbaked cookies. A hot cookie sheet can cause batter to melt and spread, which will affect the appearance of the cookies.

Mocha Toffee Crescents

Cinnamon Blossoms

Cinnamon-scented cookies are kissed with chocolate drops.

Preparation time: 50 minutes
Baking time: 8 minutes

[5 dozen cookies]

1	cup LAND O LAKES® Butter, softened
¾	cup sugar
1	egg yolk
1	teaspoon vanilla
2	cups all-purpose flour
1½	teaspoons ground cinnamon
¼	teaspoon salt

60   mini-chocolate candy kisses

1. Heat oven to 375°. Combine butter, sugar, egg yolk and vanilla in large mixer bowl. Beat at medium speed, scraping bowl often, until creamy (2 to 3 minutes). Reduce speed to low; add flour, cinnamon and salt. Beat until well mixed (1 to 2 minutes).

2. Fit cookie press with template; fill with dough. Press dough 1 inch apart onto ungreased cookie sheets. Bake for 8 to 11 minutes or until edges are lightly browned.

3. Immediately place *1* candy in center of each cookie. Remove from cookie sheets. Cool completely.

Nutrition Facts (1 cookie): Calories 60; Protein 1g; Carbohydrate 7 g; Dietary Fiber 0 g; Fat 3.5 g; Cholesterol 10 mg; Sodium 40 mg

Banana Cream Sandwich Cookies

These banana cookies are fun to make and are filled with a delicious buttery frosting.

Preparation time: 1 hour 15 minutes
Baking time: 12 minutes
Cooling time: 15 minutes

[2 dozen cookies]

COOKIE

2⅓	cups all-purpose flour
1	cup sugar
1	cup LAND O LAKES® Butter, softened
1	medium (½ cup) ripe banana, sliced ¼-inch
¼	teaspoon salt
1	teaspoon vanilla
½	cup chopped pecans

FROSTING

3	cups powdered sugar
⅓	cup LAND O LAKES® Butter, softened
1	teaspoon vanilla
3-4	tablespoons milk

Food color, if desired

1. Heat oven to 350°. Combine all cookie ingredients *except* pecans in large mixer bowl. Beat at low speed, scraping bowl often, until well mixed (2 to 3 minutes). Stir in pecans by hand.

2. Shape rounded teaspoonfuls of dough into 1-inch balls. Place 2 inches apart on greased cookie sheets. Flatten balls to ¼-inch thickness with bottom of buttered glass dipped in flour.

3. Bake for 12 to 15 minutes or until edges are lightly browned. Remove from cookie sheets immediately; cool completely.

4. Combine all frosting ingredients *except* milk and food color in small mixer bowl. Beat at medium speed, gradually adding enough milk for desired spreading consistency. Tint frosting with food color, if desired. Put cookies together in pairs with *1 tablespoon* filling for each sandwich cookie.

Nutrition Facts (1 cookie): Calories 240; Protein 2 g; Carbohydrate 31 g; Dietary; Fiber 1 g; Fat 12 g; Cholesterol 30 mg; Sodium 130 mg

Cinnamon Blossoms

Raspberry Almond Shortbread Thumbprints

This thumbprint cookie with the tang of raspberry is drizzled with an almond glaze.

Preparation time: 45 minutes
Chilling time: 1 hour
Baking time: 14 minutes
Cooling time: 15 minutes

[3½ dozen cookies]

COOKIE
1   cup LAND O LAKES®
     Butter, softened
⅔   cup sugar
½   teaspoon almond extract
2   cups all-purpose flour

½   cup raspberry jam

GLAZE
1   cup powdered sugar
1½   teaspoons almond extract
2-3 teaspoons water

1. Combine butter, sugar and almond extract in large mixer bowl. Beat at medium speed, scraping bowl often, until creamy (2 to 3 minutes). Reduce speed to low; add flour. Beat until well mixed (2 to 3 minutes). Cover; refrigerate at least 1 hour.

2. *Heat oven to 350°.* Shape dough into 1-inch balls. Place 2 inches apart on ungreased cookie sheets. Make indentation in center of each cookie with thumb (edges may crack slightly). Fill each indentation with about ¼ *teaspoon* jam.

3. Bake for 14 to 18 minutes or until edges are lightly browned. Let stand 1 minute; remove from cookie sheets. Cool completely.

4. Meanwhile, stir together all glaze ingredients in small bowl with wire whisk until smooth. Drizzle over cooled cookies.

Nutrition Facts (1 cookie): Calories 90; Protein 1 g; Carbohydrate 13 g; Dietary Fiber 0 g; Fat 4 g; Cholesterol 10 mg; Sodium 45 mg

Strawberry Lilies

Flower-shaped, butter-rich cookies are filled with ruby red strawberry jam—perfect for Valentine's Day, Easter or Mother's Day.

Preparation time: 1 hour 30 minutes
Chilling time: 2 hours
Baking time: 7 minutes

[8 dozen cookies]

1   cup LAND O LAKES®
     Butter, softened
¼   cup sugar
1   (3-ounce) package cream
     cheese, softened
1   teaspoon vanilla
2   cups all-purpose flour
¼   teaspoon salt
½   cup strawberry jam*

     Powdered sugar, if desired

1. Combine butter, sugar, cream cheese and vanilla in large mixer bowl. Beat at medium speed, scraping bowl often, until well mixed (about 1 minute). Reduce speed to low; add flour and salt. Beat until well mixed (1 to 2 minutes). Divide dough into fourths. Wrap in plastic food wrap. Refrigerate until firm (at least 2 hours).

2. *Heat oven to 375°.* Roll out one-fourth dough at a time on lightly floured surface (keeping remaining dough refrigerated) to ⅛-inch thickness. Cut with 2-inch round cookie cutter. Place 1 inch apart on ungreased cookie sheets.

3. Spoon ¼ teaspoon jam onto center of each unbaked cookie; spread to within ¼ inch of edge of cookie. Fold dough over jam to form a lily shape with thin spatula. Gently press narrow end to seal. (Jam will show at top and cookies will be cone-shaped.) Repeat with remaining dough and jam.

4. Bake for 7 to 11 minutes or until edges are lightly browned. Cool completely. Sprinkle cooled cookies lightly with powdered sugar.

*Substitute ½ cup of your favorite fruit preserves or jam.

Nutrition Facts (1 cookie): Calories 35; Protein 1 g; Carbohydrate 4 g; Dietary Fiber 0 g; Fat 2 g; Cholesterol 5 mg; Sodium 30 mg

Raspberry Almond
Shortbread Thumbprints

Crisp Peanut Butter Cookies

This classic peanut butter cookie, cross-hatched and crumbly, is too rich to really be humble.

Preparation time: 45 minutes
Baking time: 9 minutes

[5½ dozen cookies]

1   cup sugar
1   cup firmly packed brown sugar
1   cup LAND O LAKES®
      Butter, softened
1   cup creamy peanut butter
2   eggs
1½ teaspoons vanilla
2¾ cups all-purpose flour
1   teaspoon baking soda
½   teaspoon salt

1. Heat oven to 375°. Combine sugar, brown sugar, butter and peanut butter in large mixer bowl. Beat at medium speed, scraping bowl often, until creamy (1 to 2 minutes). Add eggs and vanilla; continue beating until well mixed (1 to 2 minutes). Reduce speed to low; add all remaining ingredients. Beat until well mixed (1 to 2 minutes).

2. Shape dough into 1-inch balls. Place 2 inches apart on ungreased cookie sheets; flatten in crisscross pattern with fork. Bake for 9 to 11 minutes or until golden brown. Let stand 1 minute; remove from cookie sheets.

Nutrition Facts (1 cookie): Calories 90; Protein 2 g; Carbohydrate 10 g; Dietary Fiber 0 g; Fat 5 g; Cholesterol 15 mg; Sodium 80 mg

Favorite Teddy Bear Cookies

Two-toned teddies are easy to form with this soft dough which naturally lends itself to different shapes.

Preparation time: 1 hour 30 minutes
Baking time: 7 minutes

[1½ dozen cookies]

1   cup sugar
¾   cup LAND O LAKES® Butter, softened
1   egg
2   teaspoons vanilla
2¼ cups all-purpose flour
1   teaspoon baking powder
¼   teaspoon salt
2   (1-ounce) squares unsweetened baking chocolate, melted

1. Heat oven to 375°. Combine sugar, butter, egg and vanilla in large mixer bowl. Beat at medium speed, scraping bowl often, until well mixed (1 to 2 minutes).

2. Reduce speed to low; add flour, baking powder and salt. Beat until well mixed (1 to 2 minutes).

3. Divide dough in half. Place half of dough in medium bowl. Stir in chocolate by hand.

4. For each teddy bear, form a portion of either color dough into a large ball (1-inch) for body, a medium ball (¾-inch) for head, four small balls (½-inch) for arms and legs, two smaller balls for ears. If desired, add additional balls for eyes, nose and mouth. Repeat with remaining dough, making either vanilla or chocolate teddy bears or mixing the doughs to make two-toned teddy bears.

5. To form each cookie, place large ball (body) on ungreased cookie sheet; flatten slightly. Attach head, arms, legs and ears by overlapping slightly onto body. Add nose, eyes and mouth. Use fork to make claws on paws. Bake for 7 to 8 minutes or until body is set. Cool 1 minute. Remove from cookie sheets. Cool completely.

Nutrition Facts (1 cookie): Calories 190; Protein 2 g; Carbohydrate 24 g; Dietary Fiber 0 g; Fat 10 g; Cholesterol 30 mg; Sodium 130 mg

TIP If desired, decorate cookies with frosting.

Pecan Tartlets

Stunning little pecan pies are a tempting alternative to the real thing.

Preparation time: 40 minutes
Baking time: 12 minutes

[3 dozen tartlets]

Tart Shells

1 3/4 cups all-purpose flour
1/2 cup sugar
1/2 cup LAND O LAKES® Butter, softened
1 egg
1 teaspoon almond extract

Filling

1 cup powdered sugar
1/2 cup LAND O LAKES® Butter
1/3 cup dark corn syrup
1 cup chopped pecans

36 pecan halves

1. Heat oven to 400°. Combine all tart shells ingredients in large mixer bowl. Beat at medium speed, scraping bowl often, until mixture is crumbly (1 to 2 minutes).

2. *Press 1 tablespoonful* mixture evenly on bottom and up sides of ungreased mini muffin pans. Bake for 7 to 10 minutes or until lightly browned. Remove from oven. *Reduce oven temperature to 350°.*

3. Meanwhile, combine all filling ingredients *except* chopped pecans and pecan halves in 2-quart saucepan.

4. Cook over medium heat, stirring occasionally, until mixture comes to a full boil (4 to 5 minutes). Remove from heat; stir in chopped pecans.

5. Spoon pecan mixture into baked shells; top each with pecan half. Bake for 5 minutes. Cool in pan 5 minutes; remove from pans.

Nutrition Facts (1 tartlet): Calories 120; Protein 1 g; Carbohydrate 14 g Dietary Fiber 0 g; Fat 8 g; Cholesterol 20 mg; Sodium 60 mg

[kitchen notes]

In the 1920s, sweet cream butter from Land O'Lakes was embraced by Americans, replacing the traditional 50-pound tubs from which grocers hand-packed butter at their customers' request.

Butter was also packaged in 1-pound rolls, double-wrapped in waxed paper, or in the four 1/4-pound sticks we're familiar with today. Land O'Lakes was even able to boast that its butter was favored by President Calvin Coolidge, who placed a standing order for LAND O LAKES® Butter on the presidential yacht.

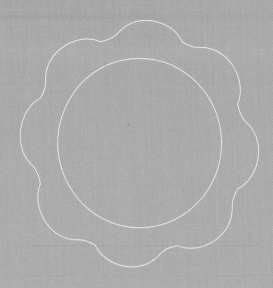

Heirloom Cookies

The elegance of traditional delicacies like rosettes or kringla gives such cookies universal appeal. While shaped cookies may take a bit more time and attention than most, they are deliciously tempting and especially appropriate during the holidays.

Hazelnut Lace Wafers

Technique

Many of these old-world treats are made with specialty irons and molds, such as krumkake and rosette irons. Look for them in Scandinavian or gourmet kitchen stores.

Sandbakkels are baked in small, fluted tins. Krumkake and pizzelle irons are hinged, like a waffle iron, and come in electric or stove-top versions.

A rosette iron is a long-handled rod with a decorative form at one end which is heated and then dipped in batter to form a delicate fried rosette.

For best results when baking tuiles or lace wafers, be sure cookie sheets are cool and lightly greased before baking. Use a wide, thin spatula to remove cookies from sheets, and work quickly when shaping; they lose flexibility as they cool.

Hazelnut Lace Wafers

A lacy-looking cookie flavored with toasted hazelnuts.

Preparation time: 45 minutes
Baking time: 6 minutes

[3 dozen wafers]

¼   cup sugar
¼   cup LAND O LAKES® Butter
3   tablespoons dark corn syrup
¼   teaspoon vanilla
½   cup all-purpose flour
1   (2-ounce) package (½ cup) hazelnuts, toasted, finely chopped

1. Heat oven to 350°. Combine sugar, butter and corn syrup in 1-quart saucepan. Cook over medium heat, stirring constantly, until mixture comes to a boil (3 to 5 minutes). Remove from heat; stir in vanilla.

2. Combine flour and nuts in small bowl. Gradually add flour mixture to sugar mixture, mixing well after each addition.

3. Drop dough by rounded teaspoonfuls 3 inches apart onto lightly greased cookie sheets. Bake for 6 to 8 minutes or until edges are golden brown. Let stand 1 minute.

4. Working quickly, loosen cookies from cookie sheets. Immediately wrap warm cookies around handle of wooden spoon, forming cone-shape. Hold in place a few seconds to form shape.

Nutrition Facts (1 wafer): Calories 40; Protein 0 g; Carbohydrate 4 g; Dietary Fiber 0 g; Fat 2.5 g; Cholesterol 5 mg; Sodium 15 mg

VARIATION

Chocolate-Dipped Hazelnut Lace Wafers
In 1-quart saucepan melt ½ cup semi-sweet real chocolate chips or vanilla milk chips and 2 teaspoons shortening over low heat, stirring occasionally, until smooth. Dip edges of wafers in chocolate. Place on waxed paper until set.

Grammie's Pfeffernüsse

These dime-sized cookies—
German for "peppernuts"—
are often flavored with a
variety of spices, including
pepper. Our version features
licorice-scented anise seed.

Preparation time: 1 hour 10 minutes
Standing time: 20 minutes
Chilling time: 2 hours
Baking time: 8 minutes

[28 dozen cookies]

¼	cup boiling water
2	tablespoons anise seed
3½	cups all-purpose flour
⅔	cup sugar
⅔	cup LAND O LAKES® Butter, softened
⅔	cup dark corn syrup
½	teaspoon baking soda

1. Combine boiling water and anise seed in large mixer bowl; let stand 20 minutes.

2. Add all remaining ingredients. Beat at low speed, scraping bowl often, until well mixed (3 to 4 minutes). Cover; refrigerate until firm (at least 1 hour).

3. Roll portions of dough on lightly floured surface into ropes ½ inch in diameter. Place ropes on waxed-paper-lined cookie sheets. Cover; refrigerate until firm (at least 1 hour).

4. *Heat oven to 350°.* Cut ropes into ⅜-inch slices. Place ½ inch apart on ungreased cookie sheets. Bake for 8 to 10 minutes or until lightly browned around edges. Store in loosely covered container.

Nutrition Facts (1 cookie): Calories 10; Protein 0 g; Carbohydrate 2 g; Dietary Fiber 0 g; Fat 0 g; Cholesterol 0 mg; Sodium 5 mg

TIP Anise was used in cooking as far back as 1500 B.C. The small annual plant is a member of the parsley family, and both its leaves and seeds are prized for their licorice flavor.

[kitchen notes]

Traditionally served at Christmastime, spice cookies, like these pfeffernüsse, are very popular in many European countries.

Norwegians make pepparnøtter, Swedes make pepperkakor and the Danes, pebernodder. These tiny cookies are rich in spices once considered worth their weight in gold: Cardamom, cinnamon, ginger and the ingredient for which all are named, black pepper.

Scandinavian Kringla

Pretzel-shaped kringla have a mild sweetness that's complemented by tea or coffee.

Preparation time: 1 hour 15 minutes
Chilling time: 4 hours
Baking time: 10 minutes

[4 dozen kringla]

KRINGLA

3⅓	cups all-purpose flour
1	teaspoon baking powder
½	teaspoon baking soda
¼	teaspoon salt
¾	cup sugar
½	cup LAND O LAKES® Butter, softened
2	eggs
2	teaspoons vanilla
⅔	cup buttermilk

SWEET RASPBERRY BUTTER

1	cup LAND O LAKES® Butter, softened
¼	cup raspberry jam
¼	teaspoon ground cinnamon

EGG WASH

1	egg
1	tablespoon water

SUGAR TOPPING

2	tablespoons powdered sugar
1	teaspoon ground cinnamon

1. Combine flour, baking powder, baking soda and salt in medium bowl. Combine sugar and ½ cup butter in large mixer bowl. Beat at medium speed, scraping bowl often, until creamy (1 to 2 minutes). Add 2 eggs and vanilla; continue beating until well mixed (1 to 2 minutes). Reduce speed to low. Alternately add flour mixture and buttermilk, beating well after each addition, until well mixed (1 to 2 minutes). Cover; refrigerate until firm (4 hours or overnight).

2. Combine 1 cup butter, raspberry jam and ¼ teaspoon cinnamon in small mixer bowl. Beat at medium speed until well mixed (2 to 3 minutes). Cover; store refrigerated.

3. *Heat oven to 350°.* Combine 1 egg and water in small bowl; mix well. Set aside.

4. Shape dough, with lightly floured hands, into 1-inch balls (dough will be slightly sticky). Roll each ball on lightly floured surface into 10-inch pencil-thin rope. Shape dough into a "U" shape on ungreased cookie sheets; carefully lift and cross ends to form pretzel shape. Brush with egg wash. Bake for 9 to 12 minutes or until lightly browned. Cool completely.

5. Just before serving, combine powdered sugar and 1 teaspoon cinnamon. Lightly sprinkle over kringla. Serve with *Sweet Raspberry Butter*.

Nutrition Facts (1 kringla): Calories 110; Protein 1 g; Carbohydrate 13 g; Dietary Fiber 0 g; Fat 6 g; Cholesterol 30 mg; Sodium 100 mg

TIP Store in airtight container with waxed paper between layers. (Surface may be slightly moist, but will dry out quickly. This helps hold the powdered sugar mixture on the cookie.)

TIP Sweet Raspberry Butter looks especially festive when served in a small ramekin or crock. Packaged together, a tin of kringla and butter in a decorative crock make a pleasing gift.

Scandinavian Kringla

Tuiles
(French Almond Wafers)

Thin and crunchy, these almond-tinged cookies are named for the rounded Mediterranean tiles they resemble.

Preparation time: 30 minutes
Chilling time: 20 minutes
Baking time: 6 minutes

[3 dozen cookies]

⅓	cup sugar
2	egg whites
½	teaspoon almond extract
⅛	teaspoon salt
½	cup all-purpose flour
⅓	cup LAND O LAKES® Butter, softened
¼	cup sliced almonds, finely chopped

1. Combine sugar, egg whites, almond extract and salt in small mixer bowl. Beat at medium speed until soft peaks form (1 to 2 minutes). Gradually beat in flour until smooth. Continue beating, adding butter 1 tablespoon at a time, until batter is smooth and well mixed (1 minute). Cover; refrigerate 20 minutes.

2. *Heat oven to 350°.* Drop batter by teaspoonfuls at least 3 inches apart onto greased cookie sheets. Spread batter, using spatula and working in a circular motion, into 1½-inch circles; sprinkle immediately with almonds. Bake for 6 to 8 minutes or until edges are lightly browned.

3. Remove cookies from oven. Press cookies over rolling pin or 12-ounce beverage can to form curved shape. Let cookies set until well formed and cooled slightly. Transfer to wire racks to cool completely.

Nutrition Facts (1 cookie): Calories 35; Protein 1 g; Carbohydrate 3 g; Dietary Fiber 0 g; Fat 2 g; Cholesterol 5 mg; Sodium 30 mg

TIP For best results, be sure the cookie sheets are cool and greased before baking tuiles. To remove the baked cookies from the baking sheets, use a wide spatula with a thin blade to avoid damaging the tuiles when transferring them to the rolling pin. Store tuiles in a loosely covered container for up to a week.

German Wreath Cookies

This is a holiday version of the traditional German cookie called Mandelbrezeln.

Preparation time: 30 minutes
Chilling time: 1 hour
Baking time: 12 minutes

[2 dozen cookies]

COOKIE

¾	cup LAND O LAKES® Butter, softened
½	cup powdered sugar
1	egg
1¾	cups all-purpose flour
½	teaspoon almond extract
¼	teaspoon salt

TOPPING

1	egg, well-beaten
¼	teaspoon almond extract
	Green decorator sugar
	Sliced almonds
	Red cinnamon candies

1. Combine butter, powdered sugar and egg in large mixer bowl. Beat at medium speed, scraping bowl often, until creamy (1 to 2 minutes). Reduce speed to low; add flour, almond extract and salt. Beat, scraping bowl often, until well mixed (1 to 2 minutes). Cover; refrigerate 1 hour.

2. *Heat oven to 375°.* Shape dough into 1-inch balls. Roll each ball into 7-inch rope on lightly floured cutting board. Shape each rope into circle, crossing ends at bottom and tucking ends under. Place 1 inch apart on ungreased cookie sheets.

3. Combine egg and almond extract in small bowl. Brush each cookie with egg mixture; sprinkle evenly with green sugar. To decorate each cookie, press 2 almond slices where wreath overlaps; press 1 cinnamon candy into center of overlap. Bake for 12 to 13 minutes or until lightly browned. Cool completely.

Nutrition Facts (1 cookie): Calories 100; Protein 2 g; Carbohydrate 10 g; Dietary Fiber 0 g; Fat 6 g; Cholesterol 35 mg; Sodium 85 mg

Serve rosettes alongside espresso or strong coffee. The delicate texture and buttery taste are the perfect foil for a rich, slightly bitter cup of joe.

Rosettes

Fragile, deep-fried pastries, buttery rosettes are made in various shapes using a special iron.

Preparation time: 10 minutes
Frying time: 25 seconds
Standing time: 30 minutes

[4½ dozen cookies]

Batter

¼   cup LAND O LAKES® Butter, softened
2   eggs
1   tablespoon sugar
¼   teaspoon salt
1   cup all-purpose flour
¾   cup milk
¼   teaspoon vanilla

1½ quarts oil (for deep frying)

Glaze

1   cup powdered sugar
1   tablespoon milk
1   tablespoon white corn syrup

1. Combine butter, eggs, sugar and salt in small mixer bowl. Beat at medium speed until creamy (1 minute). Reduce speed to low. Beat, gradually adding flour and milk, until smooth (1 to 2 minutes). Stir in vanilla.

2. *Heat oil to 375° in Dutch oven or deep fat fryer.* Heat rosette iron by placing in hot oil for 1 minute. Tap excess oil from iron. Dip hot iron into batter just to top edge of iron. (Do not allow batter to run over top of iron.)

3. Return batter-coated iron to hot oil, immersing completely until rosette is crisp and lightly browned (25 to 30 seconds). Remove from oil; allow oil to drip off. Cool completely. Repeat with remaining batter.

4. Combine powdered sugar, milk and corn syrup in small bowl; stir until smooth. Carefully dip cooled rosette edges into glaze. Allow to dry at least 30 minutes. Store in single layer, loosely covered.

Nutrition Facts (1 cookie): Calories 45; Protein 1 g; Carbohydrate 5 g; Dietary Fiber 0 g; Fat 2.5 g; Cholesterol 10 mg; Sodium 25 mg

Italian Pizzelles

These pretty wafers are served alongside scoops of gelato and sorbet in trattorias and cafes throughout Italy.

Preparation time: 30 minutes
Cooking time: 1 minute

[20 (4-inch) pizzelles]

3	eggs
3/4	cup sugar
1 1/2	cups all-purpose flour
6	tablespoons LAND O LAKES® Butter, melted, cooled
1	tablespoon baking powder
1 1/2	teaspoons ground nutmeg
2	teaspoons vanilla

1. Beat eggs in large mixer bowl on high speed until thick and lemon-colored (2 to 3 minutes). Reduce speed to medium. Beat, gradually adding sugar, until well mixed. Add all remaining ingredients; continue beating until smooth (1 to 2 minutes).

2. *Heat electric pizzelle iron according to manufacturer's directions.* Place rounded tablespoonful of batter in center of heated pizzelle iron; close lid.

3. Bake for 1 to 3 minutes or until evenly browned on both sides. Open iron; lift pizzelle off with thin spatula. Cool completely. Repeat with remaining batter. Store in loosely covered container.

Nutrition Facts (1 Pizzelle): Calories 110; Protein 2 g; Carbohydrate 15 g; Dietary Fiber 0 g; Fat 4.5 g; Cholesterol 40 mg; Sodium 120 mg

TIP To prepare these inviting wafers, you'll need a pizzelle iron. Look for one at gourmet and bakeware stores or Italian specialty shops.

TIP If using a stovetop pizzelle iron, heat iron over medium heat. (Iron is hot when a drop of water sizzles when dropped on open iron.) Place *1 rounded tablespoonful* of batter in center of heated pizzelle iron; close lid. Bake 1 minute; turn iron over. Continue baking for 1 to 2 minutes or until evenly browned on both sides. Open iron; lift pizzelle off with thin spatula.

Lemon Krumkake

Both Norwegians and Swedes make krumkake at Christmas. These thin, crisp cookies are baked in a special krumkake iron that imprints an elegant, swirled design on each cookie.

Preparation time: 1 hour
Baking time: 35 seconds

[4 dozen cookies]

3	eggs
3/4	cup sugar
1/2	cup LAND O LAKES® Butter, melted, cooled
1/2	cup whipping cream
1 1/4	cups all-purpose flour
1	teaspoon grated lemon zest

1. Beat eggs in small mixer bowl at medium-high speed until thick and lemon-colored (2 to 3 minutes). Continue beating, gradually adding sugar, until well mixed (1 to 2 minutes). Reduce speed to low. Beat, gradually adding cooled melted butter and whipping cream, until well mixed (1 to 2 minutes). Continue beating, gradually adding flour and scraping bowl often, until smooth (1 to 2 minutes). Stir in lemon zest by hand.

2. *Heat krumkake iron over medium-high heat on stovetop.* (Iron is hot when a drop of water sizzles when dropped on open iron.) Drop 1 heaping teaspoonful batter onto hot iron. Bring top of iron down gently, pressing firmly but not squeezing out batter; scrape any excess batter from edges. Bake 20 seconds; turn iron over. Continue baking for 15 to 20 seconds or until light golden brown. Open iron; lift krumkake off with thin spatula.

3. Immediately wrap hot cookie around cone or handle of wooden spoon, forming cone shape. Hold in place a few seconds to set shape. Repeat with remaining batter.

Nutrition Facts (1 cookie): Calories 50; Protein 1 g; Carbohydrate 6 g; Dietary Fiber 0 g; Fat 3 g; Cholesterol 20 mg; Sodium 25 mg

TIP Find krumkake irons in gourmet and bakeware stores or Scandinavian specialty shops.

Italian Pizzelles

English Lemon Shortbread Strips

Lemon is a flavorful complement to this traditional shortbread recipe.

Preparation time: 15 minutes
Baking time: 30 minutes
Cooling time: 15 minutes
Standing time: 30 minutes

[2½ dozen cookies]

SHORTBREAD
1   cup LAND O LAKES®
     Butter, softened
½   cup sugar
2   tablespoons lemon juice
2   teaspoons finely
     grated lemon zest
2½   cups all-purpose flour

GLAZE
½   cup powdered sugar
1   tablespoon LAND O LAKES®
     Butter, softened
1   tablespoon lemon juice
1   tablespoon finely
     grated lemon zest

1. Heat oven to 350°. Combine 1 cup butter, sugar, 2 tablespoons lemon juice and 2 teaspoons lemon zest in large mixer bowl. Beat at medium speed, scraping bowl often, until creamy (1 to 2 minutes). Reduce speed to low; add flour. Beat until crumbly (1 to 2 minutes). Knead dough until smooth by hand.

2. Press dough evenly into lightly greased 8-inch square baking pan. Bake for 30 to 35 minutes or until light golden brown. Cool completely.

3. Combine powdered sugar, 1 tablespoon butter and 1 tablespoon lemon juice in small bowl using wire whisk; mix until smooth.

4. Spread thin layer of glaze over cooled shortbread; sprinkle with 1 tablespoon lemon zest. Allow to stand 30 minutes. Cut into 2½x¾-inch strips.

Nutrition Facts (1 cookie): Calories 120; Protein 1 g; Carbohydrate 13 g; Dietary Fiber 0 g; Fat 7 g; Cholesterol 20 mg; Sodium 65 mg

Mexican Tile Cookies

A crisp almond cookie which is attractively cut to resemble tiles. When cutting out these cookies use a pastry cutter for a clean, precise edge.

Preparation time: 30 minutes
Chilling time: 1 hour
Baking time: 10 minutes

[3½ dozen cookies]

1   cup LAND O LAKES®
     Butter, softened
⅔   cup sugar
1   egg
1½   teaspoons almond extract
½   teaspoon salt
2½   cups all-purpose flour
1   egg white
1   teaspoon water
1   (4-ounce) package whole
     blanched almonds

     Sugar

1. Combine butter, ⅔ cup sugar, egg, almond extract and salt in large mixer bowl. Beat at medium speed, scraping bowl often, until creamy (2 to 3 minutes). Reduce speed to low; add flour. Beat, scraping bowl often, until well mixed (1 to 2 minutes). Divide dough into 2 equal portions; wrap in plastic food wrap. Refrigerate until firm (1 to 2 hours).

2. *Heat oven to 350°.* Roll out dough on well-floured surface, one portion at a time (keeping remaining dough refrigerated), to ¼-inch thickness. Cut into diamond shapes using pastry cutter, if desired. Place ½ inch apart on ungreased cookie sheets.

3. Beat egg white and water in small bowl until mixed. Brush over tops of cookies. Place whole almond in center of each cookie; sprinkle with sugar. Bake for 10 to 12 minutes or until edges are lightly browned. Let stand 1 minute; remove from cookie sheets.

Nutrition Facts (1 cookie): Calories 100; Protein 2 g; Carbohydrate 9 g; Dietary Fiber 0 g; Fat 6 g; Cholesterol 15 mg; Sodium 75 mg

English Lemon Shortbread Strips

Sandbakkels

A "must" on the Scandinavian cookie tray during the holidays, these delicate treasures are made in special little tins.

Preparation time: 1 hour
Baking time: 8 minutes

[3 dozen cookies]

1	cup LAND O LAKES® Butter, softened
½	cup sugar
½	cup firmly packed brown sugar
1	egg
1	teaspoon almond *or* brandy extract
2½	cups all-purpose flour

1. Heat oven to 350°. Combine all ingredients *except* flour in large mixer bowl. Beat at medium speed, scraping bowl often, until well mixed (1 to 2 minutes). Reduce speed to low; add flour. Beat until well mixed (2 to 3 minutes). If dough is too soft, cover and refrigerate at least 2 hours.

2. Press 2 to 3 teaspoonfuls dough evenly into each 3-inch sandbakkel mold. Place molds on cookie sheets. Bake for 8 to 11 minutes or until lightly browned. Cool 3 minutes.

3. Remove cookies from molds by tapping on table or loosening with knife. Cookies can be served plain or filled with fresh fruit, fruit filling, pudding or whipped cream.

Nutrition Facts (1 cookie): Calories 60; Protein 1 g; Carbohydrate 7 g; Dietary Fiber 0 g; Fat 3 g; Cholesterol 10 mg; Sodium 35 mg

TIP Sandbakkels are made in fluted tins, available in many different sizes. The most practical is two inches in diameter for tartlets small enough to serve as cookies, but generous enough to fill with a dab of jam, jelly or whipped cream. Find Sandbakkel tins at Scandinavian specialty shops, cookware and gourmet stores.

TIP If using 2½-inch sandbakkel molds, press 1½ to 2 teaspoonfuls dough evenly into each mold. Bake for 7 to 10 minutes. Yields 5 dozen cookies.

Norwegian Cookies

This cinnamon sugar cookie is perfect with coffee.

Preparation time: 30 minutes
Baking time: 13 minutes

[6 dozen cookies]

COOKIE

1⅓	cups sugar
1	cup LAND O LAKES® Butter, softened
2	eggs
1	teaspoon vanilla
3	cups all-purpose flour
1	teaspoon baking powder
1	(12-ounce) package (2 cups) semi-sweet chocolate chips

SUGAR MIXTURE

3	tablespoons sugar
¾	teaspoon ground cinnamon

1. Heat oven to 350°. Combine 1⅓ cups sugar and butter in large mixer bowl. Beat at medium speed, scraping bowl often, until creamy (1 to 2 minutes). Add eggs and vanilla; continue beating until well mixed. Reduce speed to low; add flour and baking powder. Beat until well mixed (1 to 2 minutes). Stir in chocolate chips by hand.

2. Divide dough in half on lightly floured surface. Divide each half into thirds. Shape each third into 10-inch roll. Place 2 rolls at least 2 inches apart on ungreased cookie sheet. Flatten rolls with moistened fork tines to about ½ inch thick.

3. Combine 3 tablespoons sugar and cinnamon in small bowl. Sprinkle about *1½ teaspoons* sugar-cinnamon mixture onto each roll. Bake for 13 to 15 minutes or until edges are lightly browned. While warm, slice diagonally into 1-inch strips.

Nutrition Facts (1 cookie): Calories 80; Protein 1 g; Carbohydrate 11 g; Dietary 0 g; Fat 4 g; Cholesterol 15 mg; Sodium 35 mg

Every cuisine has its sweet side. While the treats on these pages take their cues from centuries-old recipes, our modern-day versions bake, keep and serve with ease.

Lebkuchen Bars

Lebkuchen are honey-sweetened German cookies traditionally baked at Christmas. Lebkuchen keep well and taste richer as they age.

Preparation time: 20 minutes
Baking time: 18 minutes
Cooling time: 15 minutes

[24 bars]

BARS

¾ cup firmly packed brown sugar
½ cup LAND O LAKES® Butter, softened
⅓ cup honey
1 egg
1 tablespoon lemon juice
1 teaspoon finely grated lemon zest
2½ cups all-purpose flour
1 teaspoon ground cinnamon
½ teaspoon baking soda
½ teaspoon ground allspice
½ teaspoon ground cloves
¼ teaspoon ground nutmeg
⅓ cup finely chopped blanched almonds
⅓ cup chopped golden raisins

GLAZE

¾ cup powdered sugar
1 tablespoon lemon juice
1 tablespoon honey

GARNISH

Candied cherries, if desired
Whole almonds, if desired

1. Heat oven to 350°. Spray 13x9-inch baking pan with no-stick cooking spray; set aside.

2. Combine brown sugar, butter, honey, egg, lemon juice and lemon zest in large mixer bowl. Beat at medium speed, scraping bowl often, until creamy (2 to 3 minutes). Reduce speed to low; add flour, cinnamon, baking soda, allspice, cloves and nutmeg. Beat until well mixed (1 to 2 minutes). Stir in ⅓ cup blanched almonds and raisins by hand.

3. Spread batter into prepared pan. Bake for 18 to 20 minutes or until toothpick inserted in center comes out clean. Cool completely.

4. Stir together powdered sugar, lemon juice and honey in small bowl until smooth. Drizzle over bars. Garnish with candied cherries and almonds, if desired.

<u>Nutrition Facts</u> *(1 bar): Calories 180; Protein 2 g; Carbohydrate 30 g; Dietary Fiber 1 g; Fat 6 g; Cholesterol 20 mg; Sodium 80 mg*

Vanilla & Chocolate Biscotti

These twice-baked treats marry the tastes of vanilla and chocolate.

Preparation time: 25 minutes
Baking time: 37 minutes
Cooling time: 30 minutes

[3 dozen biscotti]

BISCOTTI

2	cups all-purpose flour
½	cup finely chopped walnuts, toasted
½	teaspoon baking powder
½	teaspoon baking soda
¼	teaspoon salt
1	cup sugar
¼	cup LAND O LAKES® Butter, softened
2	eggs
2	teaspoons vanilla
1	(1-ounce) square unsweetened chocolate, melted, cooled

DRIZZLE

¼	cup semi-sweet real chocolate chips
2	teaspoons shortening
¼	cup vanilla milk chips

1. Heat oven to 350°. Stir together flour, walnuts, baking powder, baking soda and salt in small bowl. Combine sugar and butter in large mixer bowl. Beat at medium speed, scraping bowl often, until well mixed (1 to 2 minutes). Add eggs and vanilla; beat until well mixed (1 to 2 minutes). Reduce speed to low; add flour mixture. Beat until well mixed (1 to 2 minutes).

2. Remove *half* of dough from mixer bowl. To remaining dough in mixer bowl add melted chocolate. Beat at low speed until well mixed (1 minute).

3. Divide chocolate dough and white dough each into two equal portions. Roll each portion on lightly floured surface into 6-inch log. Place *1 chocolate roll* on top of *1 vanilla roll*; shape into 10x1½-inch log. Repeat with second log. Place each log 3 inches apart on ungreased cookie sheet. Bake for 23 to 28 minutes or until set and lightly browned. Let cool on cookie sheets 15 minutes.

4. *Reduce oven temperature to 300°.* Cut logs diagonally into ½-inch slices with serrated knife; arrange slices, cut-side down, on cookie sheet. Bake for 14 to 18 minutes, turning once, or until crisp and golden brown on both sides. Place on cooling racks; cool completely.

5. Melt chocolate chips and *1 teaspoon* shortening in 1-quart saucepan over low heat, stirring occasionally, until smooth (1 to 2 minutes). Repeat with remaining shortening and vanilla milk chips. Drizzle over biscotti.

Nutrition Facts (1 biscotti): Calories 90; Protein 1 g; Carbohydrate 13 g; Dietary 1 g; Fat 4 g; Cholesterol 15 mg; Sodium 55 mg

TIP Biscotti can also be enjoyed plain rather than drizzled with chocolate.

TIP Biscotti are good keepers that will retain their hearty crunch when properly stored in a loosely covered container. Layered in a tin or stacked on end in a canister, they'll last for several weeks.

Vanilla & Chocolate Biscotti

Cranberry Hazelnut Biscotti

These are inspired by the cornmeal biscotti of Venice, called "zaleti," which means "little things." In Northern Italy, cornmeal is a common ingredient in desserts.

Preparation time: 30 minutes
Baking time: 39 minutes
Cooling time: 15 minutes

[2½ dozen biscotti]

BISCOTTI

2	cups all-purpose flour
½	cup (2½ ounces) hazelnuts *or* filberts, toasted, skins removed, finely chopped
½	teaspoon baking powder
½	teaspoon baking soda
¼	teaspoon salt
¾	cup sugar
2	eggs
¼	cup vegetable oil
1	tablespoon orange juice
2	teaspoons grated orange zest
1½	teaspoons vanilla
⅔	cup (3 ounces) finely chopped dried cranberries
1-2	teaspoons all-purpose flour

EGG WASH

1	egg white
1	tablespoon water
	Sugar

1. Heat oven to 350°. Combine 2 cups flour, hazelnuts, baking powder, baking soda and salt in medium bowl; set aside.

2. Combine ¾ cup sugar and eggs in large mixer bowl. Beat at medium speed until thick and lemon-colored (2 to 3 minutes). Add vegetable oil, orange juice, orange zest and vanilla. Beat until well mixed (1 to 2 minutes). Reduce speed to low. Beat, gradually adding flour mixture, until well mixed (1 to 2 minutes). Stir in dried cranberries by hand.

3. Turn dough onto lightly floured surface (Dough will be soft and sticky.) Sprinkle lightly with 1 to 2 teaspoons flour; knead flour into dough. Shape into two (8x2-inch) logs with floured hands. Place 3 to 4 inches apart on greased cookie sheets; flatten tops slightly. Combine egg white and water in small bowl; brush over top of biscotti. Sprinkle with sugar. Bake for 23 to 30 minutes or until lightly browned and firm to the touch. Let cool on cookie sheets 15 minutes.

4. *Reduce oven temperature to 300°.* Cut logs diagonally into ½-inch slices with serrated knife; arrange slices, cut-side down, on cookie sheets. Bake for 16 to 20 minutes, turning once, or until golden brown. Place on cooling racks; cool completely.

Nutrition Facts (1 biscotti): Calories 70; Protein 1 g; Carbohydrate 10 g; Dietary Fiber 0 g; Fat 3 g; Cholesterol 10 mg; Sodium 40 mg

TIP Biscotti, also called twice-baked cookies, are subtly sweet and extra-crunchy. They're perfect for dunking in cappuccino, milk, cocoa, dessert wine, and espresso. When making biscotti, be sure not to underbake the dough. Biscotti logs should be firm and not yield to light pressure when pulled from the oven. Also, make sure that the logs are thoroughly cooled before cutting into slices with a serrated knife.

TIP Toasting gives hazelnuts additional flavor and removes the bitter skin. To toast, spread nuts on a shallow pan or baking sheet and place in a 325° oven for 10 to 15 minutes. Remove and allow to cool, then slip off skins by rubbing the nuts with a kitchen towel.

Almond Spice Rugelach

These rich, cream cheese pastries are filled with almonds and rolled into delicious tiny crescents.

Preparation time: 1 hour
Chilling time: 4 hours
Standing time: 15 minutes
Baking time: 22 minutes

[4 dozen cookies]

PASTRY

2	cups all-purpose flour
3	tablespoons sugar
1/4	teaspoon salt
1	cup cold LAND O LAKES® Butter
2	(3-ounce) packages cream cheese
1/3	cup LAND O LAKES® Sour Cream

FILLING

3/4	cup finely chopped blanched almonds
1/3	cup sugar
1	tablespoon LAND O LAKES® Butter, softened
1	teaspoon ground cinnamon
1/2	teaspoon ground nutmeg

GLAZE

1	egg white, beaten Ground nutmeg, if desired

1. Stir together flour, 3 tablespoons sugar and salt in large bowl; cut in 1 cup butter until crumbly. Cut in cream cheese until well mixed. Stir in sour cream until mixture forms soft dough. Form dough into ball. Cover; refrigerate until firm (at least 4 hours).

2. Stir together all filling ingredients in small bowl; set aside. Remove dough from refrigerator; soften slightly at room temperature (about 15 minutes).

3. *Heat oven to 350°.* Divide dough into 4 pieces; form each piece into ball. Place 1 ball on lightly floured surface; flatten slightly. Roll dough into 9-inch circle, about 1/8-inch thick. Sprinkle about 1/4 cup filling mixture over dough; gently press into dough. Cut circle into 12 wedges with large, sharp knife. Roll up each wedge tightly, from wide end to point, forming crescent.

4. Place crescents, point-side down, 1 inch apart on greased cookie sheets; curve slightly. Brush each crescent with beaten egg white; sprinkle lightly with nutmeg. Bake for 22 to 25 minutes or until light golden brown.

Nutrition Facts (1 cookie): Calories 90; Protein 1 g; Carbohydrate 7 g; Dietary Fiber 0 g; Fat 7 g; Cholesterol 15 mg; Sodium 70 mg

[kitchen notes]

Rugelach are a Hannukah tradition passed down through generations. These bite-sized pastries can boast a wide variety of fillings, including raisins, poppy-seed paste, jam or nuts; the almond version we give is festive enough for a holiday table as well as a spring or autumn brunch. Made with a rich cream cheese dough and shaped into crescents, these treats are halfway between a cookie and a full-fledged dessert.

Creative Cut-Outs

Cut-out cookies are the ones we associate most with childhood memories of aromatic kitchens and wintry afternoons. Simple yet inviting, this collection of cut-outs features familiar flavors and contemporary classics—over a dozen in all.

Candy Window Cookies

Technique

Use a pastry cloth and a stockinet-covered rolling pin to make it easier to roll the dough and prevent it from sticking. Rub the flour evenly into the rolling pin cover and pastry cloth for easy handling, then roll the dough lightly and evenly before cutting the cookies.

Don't use too much flour on the rolling pin or pastry surface as it may toughen the dough.

Roll only a portion of the dough out at a time, and keep the rest covered and chilled.

To keep the dough from sticking as you make cut-outs, dip the cookie cutters in flour as you go.

Re-roll the dough as little as possible—over-handling will toughen it.

Candy Window Cookies

Charming gifts, these attractive cut-outs are just right during the holidays.

Preparation time: 1 hour
Chilling time: 2 hours
Baking time: 7 minutes
Cooling time: 15 minutes

[3 dozen cookies]

COOKIE

1	cup LAND O LAKES® Butter, softened
3/4	cup sugar
1	(3-ounce) package cream cheese, softened
1	egg
1	teaspoon vanilla
3	cups all-purpose flour

DECORATIONS

Fruit-flavored hard candies, unwrapped, finely crushed
Decorator candies
Decorator sugars

1. Combine all cookie ingredients *except* flour in large mixer bowl. Beat at medium speed, scraping bowl often, until creamy (2 to 3 minutes). Reduce speed to low; add flour. Beat just until mixed (1 to 2 minutes).

2. Divide dough in half. Cover; refrigerate until firm (2 hours or overnight).

3. *Heat oven to 325°.* Roll out dough, one-half at a time, on lightly floured surface (keeping remaining dough refrigerated) to 15x10-inch rectangle. Cut dough into 20 (3x2½-inch) rectangles using pastry wheel or sharp knife. Cut small shapes in center of each rectangle using tiny cookie cutters, hors d'oeuvre cutters *or* sharp knife. Save cut-out shapes to decorate remaining dough.

4. Place cookies on *aluminum foil-lined* cookie sheets. Fill cut-out centers of cookies with enough crushed candy to evenly fill holes. If using more than one color candy, keep candy separated by color. When filling holes, mix colors as little as possible. Bake for 7 to 9 minutes or until edges are lightly browned and candy is melted. Cool completely before removing from cookie sheets.

5. Roll second portion of dough into 15x10-inch rectangle. Cut into rectangles as directed above. Place tiny cut-out shapes of dough on each cookie. Decorate with decorator candies and decorator sugars, if desired. Bake for 7 to 9 minutes or until edges are lightly browned. Remove from cookie sheets; cool completely.

Nutrition Facts (1 cookie): Calories 100; Protein 1 g; Carbohydrate 11 g; Dietary Fiber 0 g; Fat 6 g; Cholesterol 20 mg; Sodium 55 mg

TIP To crush candy, separate candy by color. Place candy in plastic food bag. Use a hammer or flat edge of mallet to crush candy.

Lemon Sour Cream Stars

Passed on through three generations, these sour cream-lemon cut-out cookies are a holiday favorite.

Preparation time: 1 hour
Chilling time: 2 hours
Baking time: 8 minutes

[8 dozen cookies]

COOKIE

4	cups all-purpose flour
2	cups sugar
1	cup LAND O LAKES® Butter, softened
½	cup LAND O LAKES® Sour Cream
2	eggs
1	tablespoon baking powder
1	teaspoon baking soda
1	teaspoon vanilla
½	teaspoon salt
1½	teaspoons lemon extract

DRIZZLE

1	(6-ounce) package (1 cup) semi-sweet real chocolate chips
1½	teaspoons shortening

1. Combine *2 cups* flour and all remaining cookie ingredients in large mixer bowl. Beat at low speed, scraping bowl often, until well mixed (2 to 3 minutes). Stir in remaining flour by hand.

2. Divide dough into 4 equal portions; wrap in plastic food wrap. Refrigerate until firm (at least 2 hours).

3. *Heat oven to 350°.* Roll out dough, one-fourth at a time, on well-floured surface (keeping remaining dough refrigerated), to ⅛-inch thickness. Cut with 2½- to 3-inch star cookie cutters. Place 1 inch apart on ungreased cookie sheets. Bake for 8 to 12 minutes or until edges are lightly browned. Cool completely. Place on waxed paper.

4. Melt chocolate chips and shortening in 1-quart saucepan over low heat, stirring occasionally, until smooth (2 to 3 minutes). Drizzle chocolate mixture over cookies.

Nutrition Facts (1 cookie): Calories 70; Protein 1 g; Carbohydrate 9 g; Dietary Fiber 0 g; Fat 3 g; Cholesterol 10 mg; Sodium 60 mg

VARIATION
Sour Cream Cut-Outs
Omit lemon extract; increase vanilla to 2 teaspoons. Cut out dough with assorted cookie cutters into desired shapes. Bake as directed above. Frost and decorate as desired.

[kitchen notes]

A well-equipped kitchen should have several baking sheets. We suggest at least three; that way, you can rotate the sheets and bake more efficiently.

While you're filling one sheet with unbaked cookie dough, a second is in the oven, and the third is cooling off ready when you are to start the next batch.

Chocolate Mint Sandwich Cookies

A cool, creamy mint filling enlivens chocolate mint cookies.

Preparation time: 1 hour
Chilling time: 1 hour
Baking time: 6 minutes
Cooling time: 15 minutes

[6 dozen cookies]

COOKIE

1   cup sugar
1   cup LAND O LAKES® Butter, softened
1   egg
1   teaspoon vanilla
2   cups all-purpose flour
½   cup unsweetened cocoa
½   teaspoon baking soda
¼   teaspoon salt
½   cup crushed peppermint *or* spearmint candies

FROSTING

2   cups powdered sugar
¼   cup LAND O LAKES® Butter, softened
½   teaspoon peppermint extract
1-2 tablespoons milk
¼   cup crushed peppermint *or* spearmint candies

1. Combine sugar, 1 cup butter, egg and vanilla in large mixer bowl. Beat at medium speed, scraping bowl often, until creamy (1 to 2 minutes). Reduce speed to low; add flour, cocoa, baking soda and salt. Beat until well mixed (1 to 2 minutes). Stir in candies by hand.

2. Divide dough in half. Shape each half into a round; flatten to ½-inch. Wrap each round in plastic food wrap. Refrigerate until firm (1 to 2 hours).

3. *Heat oven to 400°.* Roll out dough, one-half at a time, on lightly floured surface (keeping remaining dough refrigerated) to ⅛-inch thickness. Cut with 1-inch cookie cutter. Place 1 inch apart on ungreased cookie sheets. Bake for 6 to 8 minutes or until set. Cool completely.

4. Combine powdered sugar, ¼ cup butter and peppermint extract in small mixer bowl. Beat at medium speed, scraping bowl often, and gradually adding enough milk for desired spreading consistency. Stir in crushed candies.

5. Spread about ½ *teaspoon* frosting onto flat side of *1* cookie; top with second cookie, flat side down. Squeeze together gently. Repeat with remaining cookies.

Nutrition Facts (1 cookie): Calories 70; Protein 1 g; Carbohydrate 10 g; Dietary Fiber 0 g; Fat 3.5 g; Cholesterol 10 mg; Sodium 50 mg

Butterscotch Cut-Outs

Butterscotch chips and vanilla give this cookie melt-in-your-mouth richness.

Preparation time: 1 hour
Chilling time: 1 hour
Baking time: 5 minutes

[4 dozen cookies]

1   cup butterscotch-flavored chips
3   cups all-purpose flour
1   cup LAND O LAKES® Butter, softened
½   cup sugar
½   cup firmly packed brown sugar
1   egg
2   tablespoons milk
2   teaspoons vanilla

Decorator sugars
Frosting

1. Melt butterscotch chips in 1-quart saucepan over low heat, stirring constantly, until smooth (3 to 5 minutes). Pour mixture into large mixer bowl; add all remaining ingredients *except* decorator sugars and frosting. Beat at low speed, scraping bowl often, until well mixed (1 to 2 minutes).

2. Divide dough in half; wrap in plastic food wrap. Refrigerate until firm (at least 1 hour).

3. *Heat oven to 375°.* Roll out dough, one-half at a time, on lightly floured surface (keeping remaining dough refrigerated), to ⅛-inch thickness. Cut with 2½-inch cookie cutters. Place 1 inch apart on ungreased cookie sheets. If desired, sprinkle with decorator sugars.

4. Bake for 5 to 8 minutes or until edges are lightly browned. Cool completely; frost cookies, if desired.

Nutrition Facts (1 cookie): Calories 100 g: Protein 1 g; Carbohydrate 13 g; Dietary Fiber 0 g; Fat 5 g; Cholesterol 15 mg; Sodium 45 mg

Chocolate Mint Sandwich Cookies

Triple Chocolate Wafer Cut-Outs

Crisp, double-chocolate cookies are gilded with melted chocolate.

Preparation time: 1 hour 30 minutes
Chilling time: 2 hours
Baking time: 8 minutes
Cooling time: 30 minutes

[8 dozen cookies]

COOKIE

1	cup sugar
1	cup LAND O LAKES® Butter, softened
¼	cup milk
1	teaspoon vanilla
1	egg
2¾	cups all-purpose flour
¼	cup unsweetened cocoa
1	(1-ounce) square unsweetened baking chocolate, melted, cooled
¾	teaspoon baking powder
¼	teaspoon baking soda
2	tablespoons powdered sugar

GLAZE

1	cup semi-sweet real chocolate chips*
1	teaspoon shortening

1. Combine sugar and butter in large mixer bowl. Beat at medium speed, scraping bowl often, until creamy (1 to 2 minutes). Add milk, vanilla and egg; mix well. Reduce speed to low; add flour, cocoa, melted chocolate, baking powder and baking soda. Beat until well mixed (1 to 2 minutes).

2. Divide dough in half. Wrap in plastic food wrap. Refrigerate until firm (at least 2 hours).

3. *Heat oven to 350°.* Roll out dough, one-half at a time, on lightly floured surface (keeping remaining dough refrigerated), to ⅛-inch thickness. Cut with floured 2-inch round cookie cutters. Place 1 inch apart on ungreased cookie sheets. Bake for 8 to 11 minutes or until set. Immediately remove from cookie sheets. Cool completely.

4. Melt chocolate chips and shortening in 1-quart saucepan over low heat, stirring occasionally, until smooth (2 to 3 minutes). Drizzle over cooled cookies.

* *Substitute 1 cup vanilla milk chips.*

VARIATION Omit glaze.
Decorate plain cookies using stencil with powdered sugar.

TIP Stenciling cookies is easy
and elegant. Cut acetate or waxed paper into 6-inch squares, then create or trace your design. The simpler and less complicated the design, the clearer it will appear on the cookie. Cut out the design with a scissors or sharp hobby knife, using a piece of heavy cardboard underneath. Put the paper design on the cookies that have been baked and cooled, then sprinkle with powdered sugar.

Nutrition Facts (1 cookie): Calories 50; Protein 1 g; Carbohydrate 6 g; Dietary Fiber 0 g; Fat 2.5 g; Cholesterol 10 mg; Sodium 30 mg

Kids love to help out in the kitchen. And what better project than assembling and decorating these chocolate-filled sandwiches?

Butter Mint Creams

This buttery, crisp confection blends the flavors of mint and chocolate.

Preparation time: 1 hour 30 minutes
Chilling time: 1 hour
Baking time: 6 minutes
Cooling time: 15 minutes
Standing time: 1 hour

[2½ dozen cookies]

COOKIE

1   cup sugar
1   cup LAND O LAKES®
     Butter, softened
2   egg yolks
1½   teaspoons vanilla
½   teaspoon peppermint extract
2¼   cups all-purpose flour
½   cup finely crushed starlight
     mint candies
¼   teaspoon salt

FILLING

6   (1-ounce) squares semi-sweet
     baking chocolate, melted
     Crushed starlight mint candies

1. Combine butter and sugar in large mixer bowl. Beat at medium speed, scraping bowl often, until well mixed (1 to 2 minutes). Add egg yolks, vanilla and peppermint extract. Continue beating, scraping bowl often, until well mixed (1 minute).

2. Reduce speed to low; add flour, ½ cup crushed candies and salt. Beat until well mixed (1 to 2 minutes). Divide dough in half. Wrap in plastic food wrap. Refrigerate at least 1 hour.

3. *Heat oven to 350°.* Roll out dough, one-half at a time, on lightly floured surface (keeping remaining dough refrigerated) to ⅛-inch thickness. Cut into shapes with 1½-inch cookie cutters. Place 1 inch apart on greased cookie sheets.

4. Bake for 6 to 10 minutes or until edges are lightly browned. Let stand 1 minute; remove from cookie sheets. Cool completely.

5. Put cookies together in pairs with about *1 teaspoon* melted chocolate for each sandwich cookie. Decorate as desired by rolling edges in melted chocolate, then crushed candies; dipping half of sandwich cookie in melted chocolate; or drizzling top with melted chocolate, then sprinkling with crushed candies. Place on waxed paper; let stand 1 hour to set.

Nutrition Facts (1 cookie): Calories 160; Protein 1 g; Carbohydrate 20 g; Dietary Fiber 1 g; Fat 9 g; Cholesterol 30 mg; Sodium 90 mg

TIP If desired, cut out cookies using 2½-inch cookie cutters. To assemble cookies, spread about *2 teaspoonfuls* melted chocolate on bottom of one cookie; top with bottom of another cookie.

Spicy Cardamom Crisps

Cinnamon and cardamom scents warm the kitchen while these cookies are baking.

Preparation time: 1 hour
Chilling time: 1 hour
Baking time: 7 minutes

[7½ dozen cookies]

1⅓ cups sugar
1   cup LAND O LAKES®
     Butter, softened
1   egg
2   tablespoons dark corn syrup
1   tablespoon water
1   teaspoon vanilla
3   cups all-purpose flour
1½   teaspoons baking soda
2   teaspoons ground cardamom
½   teaspoon ground cinnamon

     Sliced almonds

1. Combine sugar and butter in large mixer bowl. Beat at medium speed, scraping bowl often, until creamy (1 to 2 minutes). Add egg, corn syrup, water and vanilla; beat until well mixed (1 to 2 minutes). Reduce speed to low; add all remaining ingredients *except* almonds. Beat until well mixed (1 to 2 minutes).

2. Divide dough into thirds. Shape each third into ½-inch thick square. Wrap each square in plastic food wrap. Refrigerate until firm (1 to 2 hours).

3. *Heat oven to 375°.* Roll out dough, one-third at a time, on lightly floured surface (keeping remaining dough refrigerated), to 12 x 10-inch rectangle. Cut into 2-inch squares using pastry cutter or sharp knife; cut squares diagonally in half to form triangles. Place 1 inch apart on ungreased cookie sheets. Lightly press almonds into center of each cookie. Bake for 7 to 9 minutes or until edges are lightly browned and cookies are set.

Nutrition Facts (1 cookie): Calories 45; Protein 1 g; Carbohydrate 7 g; Dietary Fiber 0 g; Fat 2 g; Cholesterol 10 mg; Sodium 45 mg

Tea-Time Sandwich Cookies

These delicate wafer cookies are put together with a buttercream filling, forming a dainty treat for tea time.

Preparation time: 1 hour 30 minutes
Chilling time: 2 hours
Baking time: 6 minutes
Cooling time: 15 minutes

[4½ dozen cookies]

COOKIE

2   cups all-purpose flour
1   cup LAND O LAKES®
     Butter, softened
⅓   cup whipping cream
     Sugar

FILLING

¾   cup powdered sugar
¼   cup LAND O LAKES®
     Butter, softened
1   teaspoon vanilla *or*
     lemon extract
1   teaspoon grated lemon *or*
     orange zest
1-3 teaspoons milk, orange juice
     or lemon juice
     Food color, if desired

1. Combine flour, butter and whipping cream in small mixer bowl. Beat at low speed, scraping bowl often, until well mixed (2 to 3 minutes). Divide dough into thirds; wrap in plastic food wrap. Refrigerate at least 2 hours.

2. *Heat oven to 375°.* Roll out dough, one-third at a time, on well-floured surface (keeping remaining dough refrigerated), to ⅛-inch thickness. Cut with 1½-inch round cookie cutter. Dip both sides of each cookie in sugar. Place 1 inch apart on ungreased cookie sheets; prick all over with fork.

3. Bake for 6 to 9 minutes or until slightly puffy but not browned. Cool slightly; carefully remove from cookie sheets. Cool completely.

4. Combine all filling ingredients *except* milk or juice and food coloring in small mixer bowl. Beat at medium speed, gradually adding enough milk for desired spreading consistency. If desired, tint filling with food color. Carefully put cookies together in pairs with scant ½ *teaspoonful* filling for each sandwich.

Nutrition Facts (1 cookie): Calories 70; Protein 1 g; Carbohydrate 7 g; Dietary Fiber 0 g; Fat 5 g; Cholesterol 15 mg; Sodium 45 mg

Spicy Cardamom Crisps

Creamy Lemon Medallions

Luscious, lemony sandwich creams, these are lovely to serve at a backyard tea.

Preparation time: 1 hour
Chilling time: 1 hour
Baking time: 7 minutes
Cooling time: 30 minutes

[4 dozen cookies]

COOKIE

1	cup LAND O LAKES® Butter, softened
1	cup sugar
1	egg, separated, *reserve white*
2	teaspoons grated lemon zest
2	tablespoons lemon juice
1	teaspoon vanilla
2¼	cups all-purpose flour
¼	teaspoon salt
1	reserved egg white
1	tablespoon water Sugar

FILLING

2¼	cups powdered sugar
3	tablespoons LAND O LAKES® Butter, softened
1	tablespoon grated lemon zest
1	tablespoon lemon juice
1	teaspoon vanilla
2-4	teaspoons milk

1. Combine 1 cup butter and 1 cup sugar in large mixer bowl. Beat at medium speed, scraping bowl often, until creamy (1 to 2 minutes). Add egg yolk, lemon zest, lemon juice and vanilla. Continue beating, scraping bowl often, 1 minute. Reduce speed to low; add flour and salt. Beat until well mixed (1 to 2 minutes).

2. Divide dough in half. Wrap in plastic food wrap. Refrigerate until firm (at least 1 hour).

3. *Heat oven to 350°.* Roll out dough, one-half at a time, on lightly floured surface (keeping remaining dough refrigerated) to ⅛-inch thickness. Cut with 1½-inch cookie cutter. Place ½ inch apart on greased cookie sheets. Prick surface of each cookie several times with fork.

4. Stir together egg white and water in small bowl. Lightly brush surface of cookies with egg white mixture; sprinkle lightly with sugar.

5. Bake for 7 to 10 minutes or until lightly browned. Cool completely.

6. Combine all filling ingredients *except* milk in small mixer bowl. Beat at low speed, gradually adding enough milk for desired spreading consistency. Put cookies together in pairs with about *1 teaspoonful* filling for each medallion.

Nutrition Facts (1 cookie): Calories 100; Protein 1 g; Carbohydrate 14 g; Dietary Fiber 0 g; Fat 5 g; Cholesterol 15 mg; Sodium 60 mg

Mint Pastry Wafers

A refreshing chocolate mint is sandwiched between two buttery tender wafers.

Preparation time: 15 minutes
Chilling time: 1 hour
Baking time: 8 minutes

[2 dozen cookies]

COOKIE

2	cups all-purpose flour
1	cup LAND O LAKES® Butter, softened
⅓	cup whipping cream *or* half-and-half Sugar
24	thin chocolate mint wafers *or* milk chocolate squares

1. Combine flour, butter and whipping cream in large mixer bowl. Beat at low speed, scraping bowl often, until well mixed (1 to 2 minutes).

2. Divide dough in half; wrap in plastic food wrap. Refrigerate until firm (1 to 2 hours).

3. *Heat oven to 400°.* Roll out dough on well-floured surface, one-half at a time (keeping remaining dough refrigerated), to ¼-inch thickness. Cut with 2-inch round cookie cutter. Dip both sides of *each* cookie in sugar. Place *half* of cookies 2 inches apart on greased cookie sheets; place *1* mint wafer in center of *each* cookie. Top *each* with another cookie; press edges together.

4. Bake for 8 to 10 minutes or until edges are very lightly browned. Let stand 2 minutes; remove from cookie sheets.

Nutrition Facts (1 cookie): Calories 140; Protein 2 g; Carbohydrate 12 g; Dietary Fiber 0 g; Fat 10 g; Cholesterol 25 mg; Sodium 115 mg

Chocolate Holiday Miniature Cookies

These mini shortbread cookies make festive ornaments decorated with icing.

Preparation time: 1 hour 30 minutes
Baking time: 14 minutes
Cooling time: 15 minutes

[5 dozen cookies]

⅔	cup powdered sugar
½	cup LAND O LAKES® Butter, softened
½	teaspoon vanilla
1	cup all-purpose flour
2	tablespoons unsweetened cocoa
⅛	teaspoon salt

Royal Icing, if desired
(page 46)

1. Heat oven to 325°. Combine powdered sugar, butter and vanilla in medium mixer bowl. Beat at medium speed, scraping bowl often, until well mixed (1 to 2 minutes). Reduce speed to low; add flour, cocoa and salt. Beat until well mixed (1 to 2 minutes).

2. Divide dough in half. Roll out dough, one-half at a time, between two sheets of lightly floured waxed paper (keeping remaining dough refrigerated), to ¼-inch thickness. Cut with (1- to 1½-inch) cookie cutters. Place on ungreased cookie sheets. To hang as ornaments, cut small hole near edge of each cookie with end of large straw. Bake for 14 to 18 minutes or until set. Let stand 1 minute. Cool completely.

3. Outline with *Royal Icing* (page 46) as desired. Let icing dry before threading with ribbon or yarn and tying to branches of tree.

Nutrition Facts (1 cookie): Calories 25; Protein 0 g; Carbohydrate 3 g; Dietary Fiber 0 g; Fat 1.5 g; Cholesterol 5 mg; Sodium 20 mg

TIP Royal Icing hardens as it dries, making it an ideal choice for decorating. To outline cookies, use a clean, small squeeze bottle such as a mustard or ketchup dispenser, or a decorating bag. To improvise, use a heavy plastic food bag and cut a small hole across one corner. Pack icing into corner area of bag, sealing or twisting top of bag to keep out air; squeeze out icing through hole.

[kitchen notes]

Good bakers know that equipment does make a difference. For consistently successful bars, always use the pan size called for in the recipe. Bear in mind that dark pans soak up heat more quickly, resulting in a crisper surface or crust. Aluminum pans allow for excellent heat conduction and uniform browning and are often preferred for baking cookies and bars.

Buttery Jam Tarts

Luscious jam fills these tender cut-outs.

Preparation time: 45 minutes
Baking time: 12 minutes

[2 dozen cookies]

2½ cups all-purpose flour
⅔   cup LAND O LAKES®
    Butter, softened
½   cup sugar
1   egg
2   tablespoons milk
1   teaspoon almond extract
¼   teaspoon salt
¼   teaspoon baking soda
½   cup raspberry preserves

1. Heat oven to 350°. Combine all ingredients *except* raspberry preserves in large mixer bowl. Beat at low speed, scraping bowl often, until well mixed (3 to 4 minutes).

2. Roll out dough, one-half at a time, on well-floured surface (keeping remaining dough refrigerated), to ⅛-inch thickness. Cut with 2½-inch round cookie cutter. Place *half* of cookies 2 inches apart on greased cookie sheets; place *1 teaspoonful* preserves in center of *each* cookie. Make cut-out with very small cookie cutter in tops of remaining cookies. Place on top of preserves; press edges together with fork.

3. Bake for 12 to 15 minutes or until edges are lightly browned.

Nutrition Facts (1 cookie): Calories 140; Protein 2 g; Carbohydrate 21 g; Dietary Fiber 0 g; Fat 5 g; Cholesterol 20 mg; Sodium 85 mg

Snowtime Ginger Cookies

These snappy spice cookies make beautiful cut-outs and gingerbread men.

Preparation time: 1 hour 30 minutes
Chilling time: 1 hour
Baking time: 5 minutes
Cooling time: 15 minutes

[7 dozen cookies]

COOKIE
1¼ cups sugar
1   cup LAND O LAKES®
    Butter, softened
1   egg
3   tablespoons dark corn syrup
1   teaspoon vanilla
3   cups all-purpose flour
1½ teaspoons baking soda
2   teaspoons ground cinnamon
1   teaspoon ground ginger
¼   teaspoon salt
¼   teaspoon ground cloves

DECORATIONS
    Corn syrup
    Powdered sugar
    Frostings, as desired

1. Combine sugar and butter in large mixer bowl. Beat at medium speed, scraping bowl often, until well mixed (1 to 2 minutes). Add egg, 3 tablespoons dark corn syrup and vanilla. Continue beating until well mixed (1 to 2 minutes). Reduce speed to low; add flour, baking soda, cinnamon, ginger, salt and cloves. Beat until well mixed (1 to 2 minutes).

2. Divide dough into three equal portions. Shape each into round ball; flatten to about ½ inch. Wrap in plastic food wrap; refrigerate until firm (1 to 2 hours).

3. *Heat oven to 375°.* Roll out dough, one portion at a time, on lightly floured surface (keeping remaining dough refrigerated), to ⅛-inch thickness. Cut with 2- to 3-inch cookie cutters. Place 1 inch apart on ungreased cookie sheets. Bake for 5 to 7 minutes or until set. Cool completely. Decorate as desired.

Nutrition Facts (1 cookie): Calories 50; Protein 1 g; Carbohydrate 7 g; Dietary Fiber 0 g; Fat 2.5 g; Cholesterol 10 mg; Sodium 55 mg

DECORATING IDEAS

To assemble a double snowflake, spread drop of corn syrup on bottom of one cookie and attach it to top of second cookie. Let set until dry; sprinkle lightly with powdered sugar.

To stencil cookies, place stencil on cookie. Sprinkle powdered sugar evenly over stencil using small strainer. Carefully remove stencil.

To frost cookies, use Creamy Butter Frosting or Powdered Sugar Glaze. To outline cookies, use Royal Icing. Frosting recipes can be found on pages 46 and 47.

Buttery Jam Tarts

Austrian Jam Wreaths

These buttery cut-out wreaths are sweetened with your favorite fruit jam.

Preparation time: 45 minutes
Chilling time: 1 hour
Baking time: 7 minutes

[2 dozen cookies]

1	cup LAND O LAKES® Butter
3/4	cup powdered sugar
1	egg, separated
1 3/4	cups flour
1	teaspoon vanilla
3/4	cup finely chopped blanched almonds
1/2	cup sliced almonds
1/2	cup seedless raspberry *or* apricot preserves

1. Combine butter, powdered sugar and egg yolk in large mixer bowl. Beat at medium speed, scraping bowl often, until creamy (1 to 2 minutes). Reduce speed to low; add flour and vanilla. Beat until well mixed (1 to 2 minutes). Stir in finely chopped almonds by hand. Cover; refrigerate 1 hour.

2. *Heat oven to 350°.* Divide dough in half. Roll out dough, one-half at a time, on lightly floured surface (keeping remaining dough refrigerated), to 1/8-inch thickness. Cut with 2 1/2-inch round cookie cutters. Cut out 1-inch hole in half of cookies.

3. Place 1 inch apart on greased cookie sheets. Brush cookies with holes in center with reserved egg white. Top with sliced almonds; press down lightly.

4. Bake for 7 to 10 minutes or until edges are lightly browned. Cool completely.

5. Spread cookies without holes with *2 teaspoons* preserves; top with almond-covered cookies. Store in single layer.

Nutrition Facts (1 cookie): Calories 170; Protein 3 g; Carbohydrate 16 g; Dietary 1 g; Fat 11 g; Cholesterol 30 mg; Sodium 85 mg

Country Sour Cream Cookies

Passed on to three generations of moms, these cookies are a holiday favorite.

Preparation time: 1 hour
Chilling time: 2 hours
Baking time: 8 minutes

[6 dozen cookies]

4	cups all-purpose flour
2	cups sugar
1	cup LAND O LAKES® Butter, softened
1	cup LAND O LAKES® Sour Cream
2	eggs
1	tablespoon baking powder
1	teaspoon baking soda
1	teaspoon vanilla
1/2	teaspoon salt
1/2	teaspoon ground nutmeg
1/2	teaspoon lemon extract

Decorator sugars, if desired
Decorator frostings, if desired

1. Combine *2 cups* flour and all remaining ingredients *except* decorator sugars and frosting in large mixer bowl. Beat at low speed, scraping bowl often, until well mixed (2 to 3 minutes). Stir in remaining flour by hand.

2. Divide dough into 4 equal portions; wrap in plastic food wrap. Refrigerate until firm (at least 2 hours).

3. *Heat oven to 350°.* Roll out dough, one portion at a time, on well-floured surface (keeping remaining dough refrigerated), to 1/8-inch thickness. Cut with 2 1/2-inch cookie cutters into desired shapes. Place 1 inch apart on ungreased cookie sheets; sprinkle with decorator sugars. Bake for 8 to 12 minutes or until edges are lightly browned. Decorate with frostings.

Nutrition Facts (1 cookie): Calories 80; Protein 1 g; Carbohydrate 11 g; Dietary 0 g; Fat 3 g; Cholesterol 15 mg; Sodium 75 mg

If Land O'Lakes has a recipe that best represents its heritage, it must be this. Supreme in its simplicity, the frosted butter cookie is an essential in every recipe box.

Favorite Butter Cookies

This is the ultimate butter cookie, appropriate in any season.

Preparation time: 1 hour 30 minutes
Chilling time: 2 hours
Baking time: 6 minutes
Cooling time: 15 minutes

[3 dozen cookies]

COOKIE

2½   cups all-purpose flour
1   cup sugar
1   cup LAND O LAKES®
      Butter, softened
1   egg
2   tablespoons orange juice
1   tablespoon vanilla
1   teaspoon baking powder

FROSTING

4   cups powdered sugar
½   cup LAND O LAKES®
      Butter, softened
2   teaspoons vanilla
3-4   tablespoons milk

DECORATIONS

      Decorator sugars
      Flaked coconut
      Cinnamon candies

1. Combine all cookie ingredients in large mixer bowl. Beat at low speed, scraping bowl often, until well mixed (1 to 2 minutes). Cover; refrigerate until firm (2 to 3 hours).

2. *Heat oven to 400°.* Roll out dough, one-third at a time, on lightly floured surface (keeping remaining dough refrigerated), to ¼-inch thickness. Cut with 3-inch cookie cutters.

3. Place 1 inch apart on ungreased cookie sheets. If desired, sprinkle decorator sugars on some of the cookies or bake and frost later. Bake for 6 to 10 minutes or until edges are lightly browned. Cool completely.

4. Combine all frosting ingredients *except* milk in small mixer bowl. Beat at low speed, gradually adding enough milk for desired spreading consistency. Frost or decorate cooled cookies.

Nutrition Facts (1 cookie): Calories 170; Protein 1 g; Carbohydrate 23 g; Dietary Fiber 0 g;Fat 8 g; Cholesterol 25 mg; Sodium 90 mg

Buttery Pistachio Cookies

Lightly toasted pistachios give these cookies their crunch.

Preparation time: 1 hour
Chilling time: 1 hour
Baking time: 10 minutes

[6 dozen cookies]

1	cup sugar
1	cup LAND O LAKES® Butter, softened
2	eggs
2	teaspoons vanilla
$2\frac{3}{4}$	cups all-purpose flour
$1\frac{1}{4}$	cups ($6\frac{1}{2}$ ounces) finely chopped salted pistachios, toasted
$\frac{1}{4}$	teaspoon salt
1	egg white
1	tablespoon water

1. Combine sugar and butter in large mixer bowl. Beat at medium speed, scraping bowl often, until creamy (1 to 2 minutes). Add 2 eggs and vanilla. Continue beating, scraping bowl often, until well mixed (1 to 2 minutes). Reduce speed to low; add flour, *1 cup* pistachios and salt. Beat until well mixed (1 to 2 minutes).

2. Divide dough in half. Wrap in plastic food wrap. Refrigerate until firm (at least 1 hour).

3. *Heat oven to 350°.* Roll out dough, one-half at a time, on lightly floured surface (keeping remaining dough refrigerated), to $\frac{1}{4}$-inch thickness. Cut with $2\frac{1}{2}$-inch round cookie cutter; cut each round in half. Place 1 inch apart on greased cookie sheets.

4. Beat together egg white and water in small bowl. Brush tops of cookies lightly with egg mixture; sprinkle with remaining chopped pistachios. Bake for 10 to 12 minutes or until edges are lightly browned.

Nutrition Facts (1 cookie): Calories 70; Protein 1 g; Carbohydrate 7 g; Dietary Fiber 0 g; Fat 4 g; Cholesterol 15 mg; Sodium 35 mg

Twinkling Anise Stars

Decorator sugars put the sparkle in these tender anise-flavored cookies.

Preparation time: 45 minutes
Chilling time: 1 hour
Baking time: 5 minutes

[5 dozen cookies]

1	cup sugar
1	cup LAND O LAKES® Butter, softened
1	egg
1	teaspoon anise extract
1	teaspoon vanilla
$2\frac{1}{2}$	cups all-purpose flour
$\frac{1}{2}$	teaspoon baking powder
$\frac{1}{4}$	teaspoon salt

Decorator sugars

1. Combine sugar, butter, egg, anise extract and vanilla in large mixer bowl. Beat at medium speed, scraping bowl often, until creamy (1 to 2 minutes). Reduce speed to low; add flour and baking powder. Beat until well mixed (1 to 2 minutes).

2. Divide dough in half. Shape each half into round ball; flatten to $\frac{1}{2}$ inch. Wrap in plastic food wrap; refrigerate until firm (1 to 2 hours).

3. *Heat oven to 375°.* Roll out dough, one-half at a time, on lightly floured surface (keeping remaining dough refrigerated), to 1/8-inch thickness. Cut with 2-inch star cookie cutter. Place 1 inch apart on ungreased cookie sheets. Sprinkle with decorator sugars; gently press into cookies. Bake for 5 to 7 minutes or until edges are lightly browned.

Nutrition Facts (1 cookie): Calories 60; Protein 1 g; Carbohydrate 7 g; Dietary Fiber g; Fat 3 g; Cholesterol 10 mg; Sodium 45 mg

Buttery Pistachio Cookies

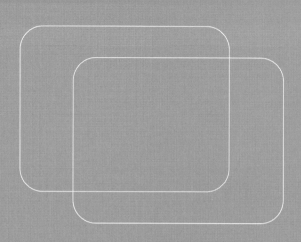

Best-Ever Bars

The simplest of all cookies to bake, bars are also infinitely satisfying. Frosted or plain, studded with treasures like chocolate and nuts or featuring hearty oats and dried fruit, the recipes on these pages squarely bring together generations of well-loved tastes.

Fudgy Raspberry Brownies

Technique

For a serving twist, try cutting bars into a new shape: For triangles, slice the bar cookies into larger squares, then cut each in half diagonally. For diamonds, make straight parallel cuts about 1½ inches apart down the length of the pan. Then make diagonal cuts about 1 to 1½ inches across the width of the pan. You may end up with odd pieces at each end. Serve as treats for those cutting the cookies.

Bars are easy to freeze. Simply remove sections of uncut, cooled bars from pan, wrap tightly in plastic wrap and store in the freezer. Defrost overnight in the refrigerator or at room temperature before cutting.

Fudgy Raspberry Brownies

Moist and rich, these bars are worthy of special occasions.

Preparation time: 15 minutes
Baking time: 40 minutes

[16 bars]

1	(6-ounce) bag (1 cup) semi-sweet baking chips
½	cup LAND O LAKES® Butter
1	cup sugar
2	teaspoons vanilla
2	eggs
1	cup all-purpose flour
¼	teaspoon salt
¼	cup raspberry preserves

1. Heat oven to 350°. Melt chips and butter in 2-quart saucepan over low heat, stirring occasionally, until smooth (5 to 8 minutes). Remove from heat; stir in sugar and vanilla. Add eggs, one at a time, mixing well after each addition. Add flour and salt; mix well.

2. Spread batter into greased 8-inch square baking pan. Drop spoonfuls of preserves over brownie; pull knife through batter for swirled effect. Bake for 40 to 45 minutes or until brownies just begin to pull away from sides of pan. Cool completely. Cut into bars.

Nutrition Facts (1 bar): Calories 200; Protein 2 g; Carbohydrate 28 g; Dietary Fiber 2 g; Fat 9 g; Cholesterol 40 mg; Sodium 100 mg

Apricot Almond Bars

This bar boasts nuts and fruit.

Preparation time: 20 minutes
Baking time: 35 minutes

[16 bars]

CRUST

1½	cups all-purpose flour
⅓	cup sugar
½	cup LAND O LAKES® Butter, softened
¼	teaspoon vanilla
½	cup sliced almonds

FILLING

1	cup apricot preserves
¼	cup sliced almonds

1. Heat oven to 350°. Combine all crust ingredients *except* almonds in small mixer bowl. Beat at low speed until mixture resembles coarse crumbs (1 to 2 minutes). Stir in ½ cup almonds by hand. *Reserve 1 cup crumb mixture; set aside.*

2. Press remaining crumb mixture on bottom of 8-inch square baking pan. Spread preserves over crumb mixture to within ⅛ inch of edge. Sprinkle with ¼ cup almonds and reserved crumb mixture.

3. Bake for 35 to 40 minutes or until crumb mixture is lightly browned and preserves are bubbly. Cool completely; cut into bars.

Nutrition Facts (1 bar): Calories 180; Protein 2 g; Carbohydrate 27 g; Dietary Fiber 1 g; Fat 8 g; Cholesterol 15 mg ; Sodium 65 mg

Peppermint 'N Chocolate Bars

Peppermint cream tops a crisp, dark chocolate cookie crust.

Preparation time: 20 minutes
Chilling time: 2 hours 30 minutes

[48 bars]

CRUST
½   cup sugar
½   cup LAND O LAKES® Butter
⅓   cup unsweetened cocoa
1   teaspoon vanilla
1½ cups graham cracker crumbs
1   cup flaked coconut
½   cup chopped nuts

FILLING
2   cups powdered sugar
½   cup LAND O LAKES® Butter, softened
2   tablespoons milk
1   teaspoon peppermint extract
3   drops green *or* red food color, if desired

GLAZE
⅓   cup semi-sweet real chocolate chips
1   teaspoon vegetable oil

1. Combine sugar, butter, cocoa and vanilla in 2-quart saucepan. Cook over medium heat, stirring constantly, until butter is melted and mixture is smooth (1 to 2 minutes). Stir in all remaining crust ingredients. Press firmly on bottom of ungreased 13x9-inch pan. Refrigerate until firm (15 to 20 minutes).

2. Combine all filling ingredients in small mixer bowl. Beat at medium speed, scraping bowl often, until smooth (2 to 3 minutes). Spread evenly over crust; refrigerate 15 minutes.

3. Melt chocolate chips and oil in 1-quart saucepan over low heat, stirring constantly, until smooth (2 to 4 minutes). Drizzle over bars. Cover; refrigerate 2 hours. Cut into bars. Store refrigerated.

Nutrition Facts (1 bar): Calories 90; Protein 1 g; Carbohydrate 10 g; Dietary Fiber 0 g; Fat 6 g; Cholesterol 10 mg; Sodium 60 mg

TIP Bars baked in a 13x9-inch pan can be cut into a variety of shapes and sizes, depending on how many servings you need. For the 48 servings suggested, cut bars in 2¼ x 1-inch rectangles. (Measure 2¼-inch segments along the short, 9-inch side of the pan, making 4 rows down the length of the pan.) For 36 servings, cut into 1½ x 2⅛-inch bars. For 54 servings, cut into 1x2-inch bars.

[kitchen notes]

Cocoa is derived from cacao liquor, an extract of the bean of the tropical cacao tree. While the spellings may be confusing, cocoa is an authentic form of chocolate that has had about half of its fat, or cocoa butter, removed.

Be sure to use unsweetened cocoa, and not instant cocoa mixes, in recipes calling for cocoa; instant cocoa contains added sugars and other granulated ingredients.

Salted Nut Bars

This bar is a new twist on old-fashioned peanut brittle.

Preparation time: 15 minutes
Baking time: 20 minutes

[36 bars]

CRUST

1½   cups all-purpose flour
¾   cup firmly packed brown sugar
½   cup LAND O LAKES®
     Butter, softened
¼   teaspoon salt

TOPPING

¼   cup light corn syrup
1   (6-ounce) bag (1 cup)
     butterscotch-flavored chips
2   tablespoons LAND O LAKES®
     Butter
1   tablespoon water
¼   teaspoon salt
1   (11.5-ounce) can (1½ cups)
     mixed nuts

1. Heat oven to 350°. Spray 13x9-inch baking pan with no stick cooking spray. Set aside.

2. Combine all crust ingredients in large mixer bowl. Beat at low speed, scraping bowl often, until mixture resembles coarse crumbs (1 to 2 minutes). Press crumb mixture into prepared pan. Bake for 10 minutes.

3. Meanwhile, place all topping ingredients *except* mixed nuts in 2-quart saucepan. Cook over low heat, stirring constantly, until chips are melted and mixture is smooth (3 to 5 minutes). Stir in nuts until well coated.

4. Spread mixture over hot, partially baked crust. Continue baking for 10 to 12 minutes or until golden brown. Cool completely. Cut into bars.

Nutrition Facts (1 bar): Calories 150; Protein 2 g; Carbohydrate 15 g; Dietary Fiber 1 g; Fat 10 g; Cholesterol 10 mg; Sodium 130 mg

Apple Pie Bars

Sprinkled with cinnamon, here's an apple pie you can eat with your fingers.

Preparation time: 45 minutes
Baking time: 45 minutes

[3 dozen bars]

CRUST

2½   cups all-purpose flour
1   teaspoon salt
1   cup cold LAND O LAKES®
     Butter
1   egg, separated, yolk beaten
     with enough milk to equal ⅔
     cup, *reserve white*

FILLING

1   cup crushed corn flake cereal
8-10 medium (8 cups) tart
     cooking apples, peeled, cored,
     sliced ¼-inch
1   cup sugar
1½   teaspoons ground cinnamon
½   teaspoon ground nutmeg
1   *reserved* egg white
2   tablespoons sugar
½   teaspoon ground cinnamon

GLAZE

1   cup powdered sugar
½   teaspoon vanilla
1-2 tablespoons milk

1. Heat oven to 350°. Combine flour and salt in medium bowl; cut in butter until crumbly. Stir in egg yolk and milk with fork until mixture leaves sides of bowl and forms a ball.

2. Divide dough in half. Roll out dough, one-half at a time, on lightly floured surface, into 15x10-inch rectangle; place in ungreased 15x10x1-inch jelly-roll pan. Sprinkle with cereal; layer apples over cereal.

3. Combine 1 cup sugar, 1½ teaspoons cinnamon and nutmeg in small bowl; sprinkle over apples. Roll remaining half of dough into 15½x10½-inch rectangle; place over apples.

4. Beat egg white in small bowl with fork until foamy; brush over top crust. Stir together 2 tablespoons sugar and ½ teaspoon cinnamon in small bowl; sprinkle over crust. Bake for 45 to 60 minutes or until lightly browned.

5. Combine powdered sugar, vanilla and enough milk for desired glazing consistency in small bowl; drizzle over warm bars. Cut into bars.

Nutrition Facts (1 bar): Calories 140; Protein 1 g; Carbohydrate 22 g; Dietary Fiber 1 g; Fat 6 g; Cholesterol 20 mg; Sodium 125 mg

Salted Nut Bars

Frosted Ginger Creams

Dense and fragrant, these spicy bars are a cross between gingerbread and gingersnaps.

Preparation time: 20 minutes
Baking time: 25 minutes
Cooling time: 30 minutes

[36 bars]

BAR
¾ cup sugar
¾ cup LAND O LAKES® Butter, softened
2 eggs
¾ cup molasses
2 cups all-purpose flour
¾ cut hot coffee
¾ teaspoon baking soda
1 teaspoon ground cinnamon
1 teaspoon ground ginger
½ teaspoon ground cloves
½ cup raisins
½ cup chopped walnuts

FROSTING
3½ cups powdered sugar
⅓ cup LAND O LAKES® Butter, softened
4-5 tablespoons milk

1. Heat oven to 350°. Combine sugar, ¾ cup butter and eggs in large mixer bowl. Beat at medium speed, scraping bowl often, until creamy (2 to 3 minutes). Reduce speed to low; add all remaining bar ingredients *except* raisins and walnuts. Beat at low speed until well mixed (1 to 2 minutes). Stir in raisins and walnuts by hand.

2. Spread batter into greased 15x10x1-inch jelly-roll pan. Bake for 25 to 30 minutes or until toothpick inserted in center comes out clean. Cool completely.

3. Combine powdered sugar and ⅓ cup butter in small mixer bowl. Beat at medium speed, scraping bowl often and gradually adding enough milk for desired spreading consistency. Spread over cooled bars. Cut into bars.

Nutrition Facts (1 bar): Calories 180; Protein 1 g; Carbohydrate 28 g; Dietary Fiber 1 g; Fat 7 g; Cholesterol 25 mg; Sodium 90 mg

Old-Fashioned Date Bars

This homestyle bar is loaded with dates and topped with crumbly oats.

Preparation time: 20 minutes
Cooling time: 30 minutes
Baking time: 30 minutes

[16 bars]

FILLING
¾ cup water
¼ cup firmly packed brown sugar
1 (8-ounce) package chopped dates

CRUST
1 cup all-purpose flour
1 cup quick-cooking oats
½ cup firmly packed brown sugar
½ cup LAND O LAKES® Butter, softened

1. Combine water, ¼ cup brown sugar and dates in 1-quart saucepan. Cook over medium-high heat, stirring occasionally, until mixture thickens and comes to a boil (4 to 5 minutes). Cool to room temperature (30 minutes).

2. *Heat oven to 350°.* Combine all crust ingredients in large mixer bowl. Beat on low speed, scraping bowl often, until mixture is crumbly (1 to 2 minutes). *Reserve 1 cup.*

3. Press remaining crumbs into greased 8-inch square baking pan. Spoon filling over crust; sprinkle with reserved crumbs. Bake for 30 to 35 minutes or until edges are lightly browned. Cool completely. Cut into bars.

Nutrition Facts (1 bar): Calories 180; Protein 2 g; Carbohydrate 29 g; Dietary Fiber 2 g; Fat 7 g; Cholesterol 17 mg; Sodium 60 mg

Can perfection be improved upon? When it comes to traditional brownies, yes. These decadent bars boast both filling *and* topping. Customize with your favorite nuts and chocolate.

Chocolate Hazelnut Brownies

Layered with sweet filling, toasted hazelnuts and chocolate, this brownie is super-rich.

Preparation time: 30 minutes
Baking time: 25 minutes
Cooling time: 30 minutes
Chilling time: 1 hour

[36 brownies]

BROWNIE
½   cup LAND O LAKES® Butter
2   (1-ounce) squares unsweetened baking chocolate
1   cup sugar
¾   cup all-purpose flour
2   eggs

FILLING
2   cups powdered sugar
2   tablespoons LAND O LAKES® Butter, softened
2   tablespoons half-and-half *or* milk
½   teaspoon vanilla
½   cup hazelnuts, toasted, coarsely chopped*

DRIZZLE
¼   cup semi-sweet real chocolate chips
¼   teaspoon shortening

1. Heat oven to 350°. Melt ½ cup butter and baking chocolate in 2-quart saucepan over medium heat, stirring constantly, until smooth (4 to 6 minutes). Stir in all remaining brownie ingredients until well mixed.

2. Spread batter into greased 8- or 9-inch square baking pan. Bake for 25 to 30 minutes or until brownies begin to pull away from sides of pan. (DO NOT OVER-BAKE.) Cool completely.

3. Combine all filling ingredients *except* nuts in small mixer bowl. Beat at medium-low speed, scraping bowl often, until creamy (1 to 2 minutes). Spread filling over cooled brownies. Sprinkle with nuts; lightly press into filling.

4. Melt chocolate chips and shortening in 1-quart saucepan over low heat, stirring occasionally, until smooth. Drizzle over filling. Cover; refrigerate at least 1 hour or until ready to serve.

5. Let stand at room temperature 15 minutes before cutting. Cut into squares. Store refrigerated.

* Substitute ½ cup salted peanuts.

TIP If you prefer, use almond extract rather than vanilla in this recipe's filling. It will lend the bars an extra touch of rich flavor.

Nutrition Facts (1 brownie): Calories 110; Protein 1 g; Carbohydrate 10 g; Dietary Fiber 0 g; Fat 6 g; Cholesterol 20 mg; Sodium 35 mg

Almond Toffee Squares

Buttery toffee and almonds are delicious partners in these simple, sophisticated bars.

Preparation time: 15 minutes
Baking time: 38 minutes

[48 bars]

1½   cups all-purpose flour
½   cup powdered sugar
¾   cup sliced almonds
1   cup cold LAND O LAKES®
      Butter
1   (14-ounce) can sweetened
      condensed milk
1   (6-ounce) package milk
      chocolate-covered toffee bits
1   egg
1   teaspoon vanilla

1. Heat oven to 350°. Combine flour, sugar and *¼ cup* almonds in medium bowl; cut in butter until crumbly. Press into ungreased 13x9-inch baking pan. Bake for 15 minutes.

2. Combine sweetened condensed milk, toffee bits, egg and vanilla in small bowl; pour over crust. Top with remaining almonds. Bake for 23 to 27 minutes or until golden. Cool completely; cut into squares.

Nutrition Facts (1 bar): Calories 140; Protein 2 g; Carbohydrate 15 g; Dietary Fiber 0 g; Fat 9 g; Cholesterol 20 mg; Sodium 90 mg

Applesauce Spice Bars

Applesauce replaces some of the fat in this sweet, spiced bar.

Preparation time: 30 minutes
Baking time: 25 minutes
Cooling time: 1 hour

[48 bars]

BAR
1   cup sugar
⅓   cup LAND O LAKES®
      Butter, softened
1   egg
1½   cups all-purpose flour
1½   cups applesauce
1   teaspoon ground allspice
1   teaspoon ground cinnamon
¾   teaspoon baking soda
½   teaspoon salt
½   cup raisins

FROSTING
2   cups powdered sugar
¼   cup LAND O LAKES®
      Butter, softened
2   tablespoons milk
2   teaspoons vanilla
⅛   teaspoon ground allspice
⅛   teaspoon ground cinnamon
½   cup chopped pecans

1. Heat oven to 350°. Combine sugar, ⅓ cup butter and egg in large mixer bowl. Beat at medium speed, scraping bowl often, until creamy (1 to 2 minutes). Reduce speed to low; add flour, applesauce, allspice, 1 teaspoon cinnamon, baking soda and salt. Beat, scraping bowl often, until well mixed (2 to 3 minutes). Stir in raisins by hand.

2. Spoon batter into greased 13x9-inch baking pan. Bake for 25 to 35 minutes or until toothpick inserted in center comes out clean. Cool completely.

3. Combine all frosting ingredients *except* pecans in small mixer bowl. Beat at medium speed, scraping bowl often, until smooth (1 to 2 minutes). Stir in pecans by hand. Frost cooled bars; cut into bars.

Nutrition Facts (1 bar): Calories 80; Protein 1 g; Carbohydrate 14 g; Dietary Fiber 0 g; Fat 3 g; Cholesterol 10 mg; Sodium 65 mg

Almond Toffee Squares

Gingered Pear Cranberry Bars

The snap of fresh ginger meets fragrant ripe pears atop an oatmeal crust.

Preparation time: 20 minutes
Baking time: 45 minutes

[16 bars]

CRUST
1¼ cups all-purpose flour
1   cup quick-cooking oats
¾   cup firmly packed brown sugar
¾   cup LAND O LAKES®
     Butter, softened
¼   teaspoon salt

FILLING
½   cup jellied cranberry sauce
1   teaspoon all-purpose flour
½   teaspoon grated fresh
     gingerroot
1   large (about 1¼ cups) firm
     Bosc pear, peeled, halved,
     cored, thinly sliced

1. Heat oven to 350°. Combine all crust ingredients in large mixer bowl. Beat at low speed, scraping bowl often, until mixture is crumbly (2 to 3 minutes). *Reserve 1 cup.* Press remaining crumb mixture into ungreased 8-inch baking pan. Bake for 15 minutes.

2. Meanwhile, combine cranberry sauce, 1 teaspoon flour and gingerroot in medium bowl; mix well. Gently stir in sliced pears to coat. Arrange pear mixture over hot, partially baked crust; sprinkle with reserved crumbs. Continue baking for 30 to 35 minutes or until crumbs are lightly browned and pears are tender.

Nutrition Facts (1 bar): Calories 190; Protein 3 g; Carbohydrate 26 g; Dietary Fiber 1 g; Fat 9 g; Cholesterol 25 mg; Sodium 130 mg

Mocha Almond Bars

Coffee gives this bar a unique flavor and almonds add a crunchy texture.

Preparation time: 20 minutes
Baking time: 25 minutes

[3 dozen bars]

BAR
2¼ cups all-purpose flour
1   cup sugar
1   cup LAND O LAKES®
     Butter, softened
1   egg
1   teaspoon instant
     coffee granules
1   cup sliced almonds

GLAZE
¾   cup powdered sugar
¼   teaspoon almond extract
1-2 tablespoons milk

1. Heat oven to 350°. Combine all bar ingredients *except* almonds in small mixer bowl. Beat at low speed, scraping bowl often, until well mixed (2 to 3 minutes). Stir in almonds by hand.

2. Press onto bottom of greased 13x9-inch baking pan. Bake for 25 to 30 minutes or until edges are lightly browned.

3. Meanwhile, in small bowl, stir together powdered sugar, almond extract and enough milk for desired glazing consistency. Drizzle glaze over warm bars. Cool completely; cut into bars.

Nutrition Facts (1 bar): Calories 120; Protein 2 g; Carbohydrate 14 g; Dietary Fiber 1 g; Fat 7 g; Cholesterol 20 mg; Sodium 55 mg

TIP Fresh gingerroot can be found in the produce section of most supermarkets. Look for gingerroot with a fresh, spicy fragrance and firm, smooth, unblemished skin. Dried, ground ginger is quite different in flavor from fresh and should not be substituted in dishes calling for fresh gingerroot. Store fresh, unpeeled gingerroot tightly wrapped in the refrigerator for up to three weeks.

Cranberry Vanilla Chip Bars

These bars are a sweet, hearty after-school favorite.

Preparation time: 25 minutes
Baking time: 25 minutes
Cooling time: 30 minutes

[16 bars]

BAR
½   cup sugar
⅓   cup LAND O LAKES®
     Butter, softened
¼   cup firmly packed brown sugar
1   egg
1   teaspoon vanilla
1   cup all-purpose flour
½   teaspoon baking powder
¼   teaspoon salt
½   cup coarsely chopped fresh *or*
     frozen cranberries
½   cup vanilla milk chips
½   cup chopped pecans, if desired

GLAZE
¼   cup vanilla milk chips
½   teaspoon shortening

1. Heat oven to 350°. Combine sugar, butter, brown sugar, egg and vanilla in large mixer bowl. Beat at medium speed, scraping bowl often, until well mixed (2 to 3 minutes). Reduce speed to low; add flour, baking powder and salt. Beat, scraping bowl often, until well mixed (1 to 2 minutes). Stir in cranberries, ½ cup vanilla milk chips and pecans by hand.

2. Spread batter into greased and floured 8-inch square baking pan. Bake for 25 to 30 minutes or until toothpick inserted in center comes out clean. Cool completely.

3. Melt ¼ cup vanilla milk chips and shortening in 1-quart saucepan over low heat, stirring constantly, until smooth (1 minute). Drizzle over cooled bars; cut into bars.

Nutrition Facts (1 bar): Calories 140; Protein 2 g; Carbohydrate 20 g; Dietary Fiber 0 g; Fat 7 g; Cholesterol 25 mg; Sodium 100 mg

TIP Fresh cranberries add wonderful flavor to these bars. If fresh are not available, frozen cranberries are an acceptable alternative. Also look for dried cranberries in the produce or bulk foods section of many supermarkets.

[kitchen notes]

Plump, shiny cranberries grow in sandy bogs on trailing vines; they're also called bounceberries because ripe cranberries will spring up with resilience when dropped.

Cultivated in Massachusetts, Wisconsin, Washington and Oregon, cranberries are harvested between Labor Day and Halloween. They are available frozen year-round.

Cranberry Macadamia Bars

Rich Macadamia nuts lend texture to this fruity, filled bar.

Preparation time: 20 minutes
Baking time: 37 minutes

[25 bars]

CRUST

²/₃	cup all-purpose flour
¹/₃	cup cold LAND O LAKES® Butter, cut into pieces
2	tablespoons sugar

FILLING

½	cup flaked coconut
½	cup (3.5-ounce jar) coarsely chopped Macadamia nuts
½	cup dried cranberries
¹/₃	cup sugar
2	eggs, beaten
1	teaspoon vanilla
½	teaspoon baking powder
¼	teaspoon salt

GLAZE

1	cup powdered sugar
1	teaspoon grated orange zest
2-3	tablespoons orange juice

1. Heat oven to 350°. Combine all crust ingredients in small mixer bowl. Beat at low speed, scraping bowl often, until mixture is crumbly (1 to 2 minutes). Press into ungreased 8-inch square baking pan. Bake for 15 to 17 minutes or until lightly browned.

2. Meanwhile, combine all filling ingredients in medium bowl; mix well. Carefully spread filling over hot, partially baked crust. Bake for 22 to 27 minutes or until golden brown.

3. Meanwhile, combine powdered sugar, orange zest and enough orange juice for desired glazing consistency in small bowl. Drizzle glaze over warm bars. Cool completely.

Nutrition Facts (1 bar): Calories 115; Protein 1 g; Carbohydrate 14 g; Dietary Fiber 1 g; Fat 6 g; Cholesterol 22 mg; Sodium 65 mg

TIP Dried fruit is a tasteful addition to this recipe. Try tossing in dried, chopped cherries or apricots instead of cranberries.

Fruit-Filled White Chocolate Brownies

Apricots, cranberries and raisins take center stage in these white chocolate brownies.

Preparation time: 45 minutes
Baking time: 51 minutes
Cooling time: 30 minutes

[25 brownies]

½	cup LAND O LAKES® Butter
1	(12-ounce) package (2 cups) vanilla milk chips*
2	eggs
¼	cup sugar
1¼	cups all-purpose flour
¹/₃	cup orange juice
½	teaspoon salt
¹/₃	cup chopped dried apricots
¹/₃	cup chopped fresh cranberries
¼	cup golden raisins
2	tablespoons firmly packed brown sugar
¹/₃	cup chopped walnuts, toasted

1. Heat oven to 325°. Melt butter in 1-quart saucepan. Remove from heat. Add *1 cup* vanilla milk chips; *do not stir.* Set aside.

2. Beat eggs in large mixer bowl at medium speed until foamy. Increase speed to high; add sugar. Beat until thick and lemon-colored. Reduce speed to low; add reserved butter and vanilla chip mixture, flour, orange juice and salt. Beat just until mixed.

3. Spread *half* of batter (about 1¼ cups) into greased and floured 8-inch square baking pan. Bake for 18 to 20 minutes or until edges are light golden brown.

4. Sprinkle apricots, cranberries, raisins and brown sugar over hot, partially baked brownies. Stir remaining *1 cup* vanilla milk chips into remaining batter; spread over fruit. (Some fruit may show through batter.) Sprinkle with walnuts. Continue baking for 33 to 38 minutes or until edges are light golden brown. Cool completely; cut into bars.

* Substitute 2 cups (12 ounces) chopped white chocolate.

Nutrition Facts (1 brownie): Calories 170; Protein 3 g; Carbohydrate 19 g; Dietary Fiber 1 g; Fat 10 g; Cholesterol 25 mg; Sodium 110 mg

Cranberry Macadamia Bars

Cappuccino Brownies

Coffee and cream flavors enliven this chocolatey confection.

Preparation time: 20 minutes
Baking time: 33 minutes
Cooling time: 30 minutes

[25 brownies]

BROWNIE

1	tablespoon instant espresso powder
2	teaspoons hot water
1	cup semi-sweet real chocolate chips
½	cup LAND O LAKES® Butter
1	cup sugar
1	teaspoon vanilla
2	eggs
1	cup all-purpose flour
½	teaspoon baking powder
¼	teaspoon salt

FROSTING

1	teaspoon instant espresso powder
2-3	tablespoons milk *or* cream
2	cups powdered sugar
¼	cup LAND O LAKES® Butter, softened

DRIZZLE

⅓	cup semi-sweet real chocolate chips
½	teaspoon shortening

1. Heat oven to 350°. Combine 1 tablespoon espresso powder and hot water in small bowl; stir to dissolve. Set aside.

2. Melt 1 cup chocolate chips and ½ cup butter in 3-quart saucepan over low heat, stirring occasionally, until smooth (4 to 7 minutes). Remove from heat; stir in espresso mixture, sugar and vanilla. Add eggs, one at a time, mixing well after each addition. Add flour, baking powder and salt; stir until well mixed.

3. Spread mixture into greased 8-inch square baking pan. Bake for 33 to 38 minutes or until brownies just begin to pull away from sides of pan. (DO NOT OVER-BAKE.) Cool completely.

4. Combine 1 teaspoon espresso powder and 2 tablespoons milk in small mixer bowl; stir to dissolve. Add powdered sugar and ¼ cup butter. Beat at low speed, scraping bowl often and adding additional milk if necessary, to reach desired spreading consistency. Frost cooled brownies.

5. Melt ⅓ cup chocolate chips and shortening in 1-quart saucepan over low heat, stirring occasionally, until smooth (2 to 4 minutes).

6. Drizzle chocolate over frosting; swirl with toothpick or knife for marbled effect.

Nutrition Facts (1 brownie): Calories 180; Protein 2 g; Carbohydrate 28 g; Dietary Fiber 1 g; Fat 9 g; Cholesterol 34 mg; Sodium 95 mg

TIP For perfect brownies, follow these simple guidelines: Don't over-beat, which can cause brownies to rise too quickly when baking—as they cool, they will fall. Instead, beat ingredients just enough to mix, then spoon into baking pan. Also be careful not to over-bake brownies; remove from oven when brownies just begin to pull away from the sides of the pan.

Cappuccino Brownies

Cookie Contest

Every family has its signature cookies—recipes handed down through the generations or conjured up in a moment of kitchen inspiration. After combing the country and meeting thousands of wonderful families —and cookies—everywhere we went, we did the hard work of paring down to just 10 recipes. Presenting this year's National Cookie Contest winners, with our thanks to all those who participated.

Giant Toffee Pecan Cookies, page 119

National Cookie Contest

Over the past year, the Land O'Lakes kitchen literally went on the road, traveling across the country in search of cookie perfection. At each stop, families brought us their treasured recipes, told us their stories and sampled Land O'Lakes' own signature family recipe, Raspberry Almond Shortbread Thumbprint Cookies (see page 60).

Ten families' cookies were selected as this year's Cookie Contest winners. We're delighted to share their treasured recipes with you.

Brown Sugar Cashew Cookies

This is my family's favorite cookie. I always make them for Thanksgiving and my husband requests these instead of birthday cake. Almost everyone who tries them asks for the recipe. I was given the recipe many years ago by a farm wife who moved next door to me. She has since passed away, but I always think of her when I make these cookies.
—Susan McNamara, Farmington, MN

Preparation time: 1 hour 10 minutes
Baking time: 10 minutes

[3½ dozen cookies]

COOKIE
1   cup firmly packed brown sugar
½   cup LAND O LAKES® Butter, softened
1   egg
1   teaspoon vanilla
2   cups all-purpose flour
¾   teaspoon baking powder
¾   teaspoon baking soda
⅓   cup LAND O LAKES® Sour Cream
1¾   cups cashew halves

     cashew halves, if desired

FROSTING
½   cup LAND O LAKES® Butter
2   cups powdered sugar
3   tablespoons milk
1   teaspoon vanilla

1. Heat oven to 350°. Combine brown sugar and ½ cup butter in large mixer bowl. Beat at medium speed, scraping bowl often, until creamy (1 to 2 minutes). Add egg and vanilla; continue beating until well mixed (1 to 2 minutes).

2. Reduce speed to low. Beat, adding flour, baking powder, and baking soda alternately with sour cream until well mixed (1 to 2 minutes). Stir in cashews by hand.

3. Drop dough by level tablespoonfuls 2 inches apart onto ungreased cookie sheets. Bake for 10 to 12 minutes or until golden brown. Cool completely.

4. Melt ½ cup butter in heavy 1-quart saucepan over medium heat. Continue cooking, stirring occasionally, until butter foams and just starts to turn golden (4 to 6 minutes). (WATCH CLOSELY.) Immediately remove from heat. Pour into medium bowl; cool 5 minutes.

5. Add powdered sugar, milk and vanilla; beat until smooth. Frost cooled cookies. Top each cookie with cashew half, if desired.

Nutrition Facts (1 cookie): Calories 140; Protein 2 g; Carbohydrate 17 g; Dietary Fiber 0 g; Fat 8 g; Cholesterol 20 mg; Sodium 115 mg

Maple Butter Pecan Shortbread

⭐ *This recipe is a special family baking tradition because every Christmas my grandmother and I made a similar shortbread cookie. I lost my grandmother's original recipe and this is the recreation. Smelling these cookies baking reminds me of my grandmother's house.*
—Jody Issod, Marlborough, MA

Preparation time: 15 minutes
Baking time: 32 minutes

[25 bars]

SHORTBREAD
½   cup LAND O LAKES®
      Butter, softened
⅓   cup firmly packed brown sugar
1   cup all-purpose flour

TOPPING
⅓   cup firmly packed brown sugar
3   tablespoons pure maple syrup
1   egg
½   cup finely chopped pecans

1. Heat oven to 350°. Combine butter and ⅓ cup brown sugar in small mixer bowl. Beat at medium speed, scraping bowl often, until creamy (1 to 2 minutes). Reduce speed to low; add flour. Beat, scraping bowl often, until mixture forms a dough (2 to 3 minutes). Press evenly into ungreased 8-inch square baking pan. Prick with fork. Bake for 20 minutes.

2. Meanwhile, combine ⅓ cup brown sugar, maple syrup and egg in small bowl; mix well.

3. Spread topping over hot, partially baked shortbread; sprinkle with pecans. Continue baking for 12 to 16 minutes or until lightly browned. Immediately run knife around edges to loosen. Cool completely. Cut into bars.

Nutrition Facts *(1 bar):* Calories 100; Protein 1 g; Carbohydrate 12 g; Dietary Fiber 0 g; Fat 6 g; Cholesterol 20 mg; Sodium 45 mg

Giant Toffee Pecan Cookies (The Big One)

⭐ *The recipe is a favorite in my family, especially my six-year-old daughter, Sarah. Every time I would make cookies, she'd always say, "Mommy, will you make the BIG ONE? They're my favorite!" So we started to call these "The Big One."*
—Denise Myres, Fayetteville, NC

Preparation time: 40 minutes
Baking time: 11 minutes

[20 cookies]

1   cup LAND O LAKES®
        Butter, softened
¾   cup firmly packed brown sugar
½   cup sugar
2   eggs
1   tablespoon vanilla
2¼   cups all-purpose flour
2   teaspoons baking powder
½   teaspoon salt
1   (12-ounce) package (2 cups)
        semi-sweet chocolate chips
¾   cup chopped pecans
⅔   cup English toffee chips

1. Heat oven to 350°. Combine butter, brown sugar and sugar in large mixer bowl. Beat at medium speed, scraping bowl often, until creamy (1 to 2 minutes). Add eggs and vanilla; continue beating until well mixed (1 to 2 minutes). Reduce speed to low; add flour, baking powder and salt. Beat until well mixed (1 to 2 minutes). Stir in chocolate chips, pecans and toffee chips by hand.

2. Drop dough by ¼-cupfuls 2 inches apart onto ungreased cookie sheets. Bake for 11 to 16 minutes or until edges are lightly browned. Let stand 2 minutes; remove from cookie sheets.

Nutrition Facts *(1 cookie):* Calories 320; Protein 3 g; Carbohydrate 37 g; Dietary Fiber 2 g; Fat 19 g; Cholesterol 50 mg; Sodium 210 mg

TIP Cookies will look underbaked in center but will continue to brown while cooling.

Fickles Shortbread

 This is a classic shortbread cookie dough in one of the many ways I make it. I call it "Fickles," because by changing the nuts, chips or flavorings, you can make just about anything you want. This is one my family particularly likes. I have made a zillion of them.
—Shirley Kacmarik, Binghamton, NY

Preparation time: 20 minutes
Baking time: 20 minutes

[48 bars]

SHORTBREAD
1   cup LAND O LAKES®
    Butter, softened
½   cup sugar
2   cups all-purpose flour
½   cup finely chopped walnuts
½   cup toffee chips

GLAZE
1   cup powdered sugar
1½ teaspoons vanilla
2-3 tablespoons milk

1. Heat oven to 350°. Combine butter and sugar in large mixer bowl. Beat at medium speed, scraping bowl often, until creamy (1 to 2 minutes). Reduce speed to low; add flour. Beat until mixture forms a dough (2 to 3 minutes). Stir in walnuts and toffee chips by hand.

2. Press dough evenly into ungreased 15x10 x1-inch jelly-roll pan. Bake for 20 to 24 minutes or until golden brown. Cut into diamond or rectangle shape while hot. Cool 5 minutes.

3. Meanwhile, combine powdered sugar and vanilla in small bowl. Gradually stir in enough milk for desired glazing consistency. Spread over warm shortbread. Cool completely.

Nutrition Facts (1 bar): Calories 80; Protein 1 g; Carbohydrate 9 g; Dietary Fiber 0 g; Fat 5 g; Cholesterol 10 mg; Sodium 40 mg

Drizzled Oatmeal Cookies

My most vivid memory of visiting Grandma's house is the smell of her freshly baked, drizzled oatmeal cookies as I walked through the door. As I grew older, I begged her to wait for me to bake the cookies. I felt special to have a hand in baking a cookie the whole family raved about.
—Megan Schnelle, Marietta, GA

Preparation time: 30 minutes
Baking time: 12 minutes
Cooling time: 15 minutes

[2 dozen cookies]

COOKIE
1   cup firmly packed brown sugar
1   cup LAND O LAKES®
     Butter, softened
¼   cup water
2½   cups uncooked old-fashioned
     rolled *or* quick-cooking oats
1¼   cups all-purpose flour
1   teaspoon ground cinnamon
½   teaspoon baking soda
¼   teaspoon salt

DRIZZLE
1   cup powdered sugar
3   tablespoons unsweetened
     cocoa
1   teaspoon LAND O LAKES®
     Butter, softened
2-3 tablespoons milk

1. Heat oven to 350°. Combine brown sugar and 1 cup butter in large mixer bowl. Beat at medium speed, scraping bowl often, until creamy (1 to 2 minutes). Add water; continue beating until well mixed (1 to 2 minutes).

2. Reduce speed to low; add oats, flour, cinnamon, baking soda and salt. Beat until well mixed (1 to 2 minutes).

3. Shape dough into 1½-inch balls. (Dough will be sticky.) Place 2 inches apart on ungreased cookie sheets. Flatten to 2-inch diameter with bottom of glass dipped in sugar. Bake for 12 to 15 minutes or until lightly browned. Let stand 1 minute; remove from cookie sheets. Cool completely.

4. Combine all drizzle ingredients *except* milk in small mixer bowl. Beat at low speed, scraping bowl often and gradually adding enough milk for desired drizzling consistency. Drizzle over cooled cookies.

Nutrition Facts (1 cookie): Calories 180; Protein 2 g; Carbohydrate 25 g; Dietary Fiber 1 g; Fat 9 g; Cholesterol 20 mg; Sodium 135 mg

Brown Sugar Cashew
Cookies, page 118
Drizzled Oatmeal Cookies
Fickles Shortbread

Raspberry White Chocolate Bars

⭐ *Because my husband lost the grocery list on his way to the store, he tried to remember what was on it. He came home with the wrong ingredients. I changed the recipe completely, using what he bought, and now as we devour these we laugh at his great mistake.*
—Julie Rhyne, Houston, TX

Preparation time: 15 minutes
Baking time: 50 minutes

[48 bars]

1½	cups sugar
1½	cups LAND O LAKES® Butter, softened
1	teaspoon salt
2	teaspoons vanilla
4	cups all-purpose flour
2	eggs
1	(18-ounce) jar red raspberry preserves
1	cup vanilla milk chips

1. Heat oven to 350°. Combine sugar, butter, salt and vanilla in large mixer bowl. Beat at medium speed, scraping bowl often, until well mixed (1 to 2 minutes). Reduce speed to low. Beat, adding flour 1 cup at a time and scraping bowl often, until mixture is crumbly (1 to 2 minutes). *Remove 1 cup of crumb mixture*; set aside.

2. Add eggs to remaining crumb mixture in bowl; beat until mixture forms a dough (1 to 2 minutes). Press dough evenly into ungreased 13x9-inch baking pan. Bake for 30 minutes or until lightly browned.

3. Spread preserves over hot, partially baked bars. Sprinkle vanilla chips over preserves. Sprinkle with reserved crumb mixture.

4. Continue baking for 20 to 25 minutes or until topping is lightly browned. Cool completely. Cut into bars.

Nutrition Facts (1 bar): Calories 160; Protein 2 g; Carbohydrate 23 g; Dietary Fiber 0 g; Fat 7 g; Cholesterol 25 mg; Sodium 115 mg

Geri's Frosted Ginger Cookies

⭐ *My mom prepared these mouth-watering cookies when I was growing up, and now I make them for my family. The wonderful aroma of these soft, delicious cookies baking makes a house smell like home. And you guessed it—they disappear fast!*
—Geri Barta, Huron, SD

Preparation time: 1 hour 25 minutes
Baking time: 10 minutes
Cooling time: 15 minutes

[6 dozen cookies]

COOKIE

1½	cups LAND O LAKES® Butter, softened
1	cup sugar
1	cup firmly packed brown sugar
½	cup light molasses
2	eggs
2	teaspoons vanilla
4½	cups all-purpose flour
1	tablespoon ground ginger
1	teaspoon baking soda
1	teaspoon ground cinnamon
½	teaspoon salt
½	teaspoon ground cloves

FROSTING

⅓	cup firmly packed brown sugar
¼	cup milk
2	tablespoons LAND O LAKES® Butter, softened
2	cups powdered sugar
½	teaspoon vanilla

1. Heat oven to 325°. Combine 1½ cups butter, sugar and 1 cup brown sugar in large mixer bowl. Beat at medium speed, scraping bowl often, until creamy (1 to 2 minutes). Add molasses, eggs, and 2 teaspoons vanilla; continue beating until smooth (1 to 2 minutes). Reduce speed to Low; add all remaining cookie ingredients. Beat until well mixed (1 to 2 minutes).

2. Drop dough by rounded table-spoonfuls 2 inches apart onto ungreased cookie sheets. Bake for 10 to 12 minutes or until cookies spring back when touched lightly in center. (DO NOT OVER-BAKE.) Let stand 1 minute; remove from cookie sheets. Cool completely.

3. Cook ⅓ cup brown sugar, milk and 2 tablespoons butter in 2-quart saucepan over medium heat, stirring occasionally, until mixture comes to a boil (3 to 4 minutes). Remove from heat. Add powdered sugar and ½ teaspoon vanilla; beat until well mixed. Cool until mixture reaches desired spreading consistency (5 to 10 minutes). Frost cooled cookies.

Nutrition Facts (1 cookie): Calories 110; Protein 1 g; Carbohydrate 18 g; Dietary Fiber 0 g; Fat 4.5 g; Cholesterol 15 mg; Sodium 80 mg

Frosted Banana Cookies

My family has always been fond of bananas. It seemed I always had a couple left over that were too ripe to eat. I worked on ways to use these and came up with this recipe after many unsuccessful attempts at creating a banana cookie that was tasty.
—Maxine Henderson, Ypsilanti, MI

Preparation time: 1 hour
Baking time: 8 minutes
Cooling time: 15 minutes

[4 dozen cookies]

COOKIE

¾ cup firmly packed brown sugar
¾ cup LAND O LAKES® Butter, softened
2 medium (⅔ cup) ripe bananas, mashed
1 egg
2 teaspoons grated orange peel
½ teaspoon vanilla
2 cups all-purpose flour
½ teaspoon baking powder
½ teaspoon baking soda
¼ teaspoon salt

GLAZE

2 tablespoons LAND O LAKES® Butter
3 tablespoons firmly packed brown sugar
3 tablespoons whipping cream*
1 cup powdered sugar
½ teaspoon vanilla

1. Heat oven to 350°. Combine ¾ cup brown sugar and ¾ cup butter in large mixer bowl. Beat at medium speed, scraping bowl often, until creamy (1 to 2 minutes). Add bananas, egg, orange zest, and ½ teaspoon vanilla; continue beating until well mixed (1 to 2 minutes).

2. Reduce speed to low; add flour, baking powder, baking soda and salt. Beat until well mixed (1 to 2 minutes).

3. Drop dough by rounded teaspoonfuls 2 inches apart onto ungreased cookie sheets. Bake for 8 to 10 minutes or until edges are lightly browned. Cool completely.

4. Melt 2 tablespoons butter in 1-quart saucepan over medium heat. Add 3 tablespoons brown sugar and whipping cream. Continue cooking, stirring occasionally, until mixture comes to a boil (1 to 2 minutes). Remove from heat. Add powdered sugar and ½ teaspoon vanilla; beat until well mixed (1 to 2 minutes). Frost cooled cookies.

* Substitute half-and-half or milk. After beating in powdered sugar, let cool to desired spreading consistency (5 to 10 minutes).

Nutrition Facts (1 cookie): Calories 80; Protein 1 g; Carbohydrate 11 g; Dietary Fiber 0 g; Fat 4 g; Cholesterol 15 mg ; Sodium 65 mg

Slice & Bake
Cinnamon Crisps

I rescued this recipe from an old, tattered, hand-written book belonging to my mother-in-law when she died. Oldest in a family of ten, she knew all there was to know about cooking and baking. This was one of her Christmas favorites. So rich and buttery—absolutely delicious!
—Mary Malchow, Neenah, WI

Preparation time: 40 minutes
Chilling time: 1 hour
Baking time: 7 minutes

[5 dozen cookies]

1   cup LAND O LAKES®
       Butter, softened
½   cup firmly packed brown sugar
1   teaspoon vanilla
2¼   cups all-purpose flour
½   cup sugar
1   teaspoon ground cinnamon

1. Combine butter, brown sugar and vanilla in large mixer bowl. Beat at medium speed, scraping bowl often, until creamy (1 to 2 minutes). Reduce speed to low; add flour. Beat, scraping bowl often, until mixture forms a dough (2 to 5 minutes).

2. Divide dough into fourths. Shape each fourth into 4x1½-inch roll. Flatten roll to form triangle or square shape. Wrap each roll in plastic food wrap; refrigerate at least 1 hour.

3. *Heat oven to 375°.* Cut rolls into ¼-inch slices with sharp knife.

Place 1 inch apart on ungreased cookie sheets. Bake 7 to 9 minutes or until lightly browned on edges. Cool slightly.

4. Stir together sugar and cinnamon in small bowl. Roll warm cookies in cinnamon-sugar mixture.

Nutrition Facts (1 cookie): Calories 60; Protein 1 g; Carbohydrate 7 g; Dietary Fiber 0 g; Fat 3 g; Cholesterol 10 mg; Sodium 30 mg

Chocolate
Sandwich Cookies

My mother's friend brought these cookies to a farewell celebration for my brother. I asked my mother to get the recipe; she thought it was a guarded secret when she didn't succeed. Years later, to my surprise and utter delight, it appeared in my mail in her friend's handwriting.
—Trudy Russell, Iowa City, IA

Preparation time: 1 hour 15 minutes
Baking time: 6 minutes
Cooling time: 15 minutes

[4 dozen sandwich cookies]

COOKIE
1½   cups firmly packed
       brown sugar
¾   cup LAND O LAKES® Butter
2   tablespoons water
1   (12-ounce) package (2 cups)
       semi-sweet real chocolate chips
2   eggs
3   cups all-purpose flour
1¼   teaspoons baking soda
1   teaspoon salt

FILLING
3   cups powdered sugar
⅓   cup LAND O LAKES®
       Butter, softened
1   teaspoon vanilla
2-4   tablespoons milk

1. Heat oven to 350°. Combine brown sugar, ¾ cup butter and water in heavy 3-quart saucepan. Cook over medium heat, stirring occasionally, until butter is melted (3 to 4 minutes). Add chocolate chips; continue cooking, stirring constantly, until chocolate is melted and smooth (1 to 2 minutes). Remove from heat. Beat in eggs, one at a time, until mixture is smooth. Stir in all remaining cookie ingredients.

2. Drop dough by rounded tea-spoonfuls onto ungreased cookie sheets. Bake for 6 to 8 minutes or until set. Let stand 1 minute; remove from cookie sheets. Cool completely.

3. Meanwhile, combine all filling ingredients *except* milk in large mixer bowl. Beat at low speed, scraping bowl often and gradually adding enough milk for desired spreading consistency.

4. Spread about *2 teaspoons* frosting onto flat-side of one cookie; top with second cookie, flat-side down. Squeeze together gently. Repeat with remaining cookies.

Nutrition Facts (1 sandwich cookie): Calories 160 ; Protein 1 g; Carbohydrate 25 g; Dietary Fiber 1 g; Fat 7 g; Cholesterol 20 mg; Sodium 125 mg

Chocolate Sandwich Cookies
Geri's Frosted Ginger Cookies, page 122
Slice & Bake Cinnamon Crisps

Index